How to Back Up a Trailer

How to Back Up a Trailer

...AND **101** OTHER THINGS
EVERY **REAL GUY** SHOULD KNOW

Kurt Anderson

Aadamsmedia
Avon, Massachusetts

Published by
Adams Media, a division of F+W Media, Inc.
57 Littlefield Street, Avon, MA 02322. U.S.A.
www.adamsmedia.com

ISBN 10: 1-59869-493-6
ISBN 13: 978-1-59869-493-2

Printed in the United States of America.

10   9   8   7   6   5   4   3

Library of Congress Cataloging-in-Publication Data
is available from the publisher.

Interior illustrations by Eric Andrews.

This book is available at quantity discounts for bulk purchases.
For information, please call 1-800-289-0963.

This book is dedicated in loving memory of my father, Bill Anderson, who left this world a few years back. He is still with me, though . . . and no doubt laughing, in his good way, when I'm being a knuckle-head about one thing or another.

Miss you, Dad.

William "Bill" Anderson. 1941–2004

CONTENTS

SECTION 2 **Sporting...43**

Contents

SECTION 3 **Outdoors...87**

SECTION 4 **Household and Garage...137**

SECTION 5 **Social...159**

Contents

ACKNOWLEDGMENTS

I'd like to thank the following people for their help with this book:

To Justin Neudahl, longtime supporter, an invaluable first reader, and duck-blind buddy, I owe many thanks, most of all for being a friend. The other guys and gals from whom I've learned "real-guy" stuff could fill up pages, but I'd especially like to thank Adam Janke, Willy Janke, the Ehnes clan, Robert "Button Buck" Anderson, Wayno Langley, Don "Corky" Hemsworth, Kurt Johnson, Todd Blom, Rick McRae, and Al Price. To my sisters, Suzie Janke and Becca Karppinen, and my mother, Nita Anderson, thanks for everything, and especially for putting up with "Cliff." You know what I mean.

Sometimes the simplest things take on a new wonder when you show them to, or experience them with, fresh eyes: Kolten, Kourtney, Kody, Krystal, Drew, Lindsey, and Joey, you guys (and girls) rock.

I'd also like to thank Duane Johnson and Gary Wentz at *The Family Handyman* magazine, two of the nicest guys out there. Their guidance in how-to writing was indispensable. Thanks many times over to Jill Alexander and Katrina Schroeder for their enthusiasm and help in shaping an idea into a book.

This book would not have happened without Jim Donovan, one hell of a fine literary agent and person. Many thanks, chief.

And most importantly, I'd like to express my gratitude to my wife, Tina Lee, for keeping an eye on our wonderful sons, Tyler and Carter, while I was writing, for always encouraging me, and for being the best wife a guy could ask for. Love ya, hon.

INTRODUCTION

Here's a shocker: Guys don't know everything. In fact, when it comes to supposedly "innate" guy knowledge, a lot of us feel like we're holding a weak flashlight in a big, dark garage, just trying to figure out how to open up the damn overhead door.

We stand, as the saying goes, on the shoulders of geniuses. Our mechanically ingenious fathers and grandfathers left us a world of complicated machinery in their wake, willing us an incredible amount of "should-know" technical detail, on everything from electricity to ballistics to physics. Along with the practical stuff, we also inherited arcane yet still-powerful rules of sportsmanship and hard-nosed etiquette, with nuances and intricacies as unfathomable as three-fork place settings. But those geniuses didn't leave us a guidebook—or even an instruction manual. No wonder we feel lost from time to time.

It's hard to admit this, especially if you're a guy. We like and admire those handy types who can fix a shoulder-stalled car or rewire a faulty light switch, those practical men who know how to clean a fish and make a smokeless fire to cook it over. We want to be like them, to have that natural confidence that shows through so plainly, even when—maybe *especially* when—things start going to hell.

Well, nobody is born knowing how to shuffle cards or fillet a fish, and even the most experienced mechanic was probably baffled the first time he changed oil. Unless, of course, someone showed him the way first. And if there was nobody there to show him the way, he went ahead and figured it out all by himself. In an increasingly busy world, and one in which fathers are not always around, learning stuff yourself sometimes seems like the only option.

Well, learning things the hard way can be both entertaining and memorable. Yet I've suffered enough broken bones and bruises on my ego to realize that sometimes the hard way is, well, just *hard*, with no redeeming value. It doesn't hurt to take a little advice now and then, because this isn't stuff we're born with.

But it is stuff you should know.

This book is a guide into the world of real guys, a fascinating place full of hidden secrets and clever solutions, a world that everyone, man or woman, should at least visit from time to time. I've learned these things on the water and in the garage, from strangers and friends and, most importantly, from my dad. I've been lucky—I've known some incredible people. They've shown me some incredible stuff, and I've learned a few things on my own, too.

Still, it hasn't always been a smooth ride. In the following pages, you'll see plenty of ways to screw things up, even when you think you know what you're doing. There are a couple ways to deal with these failure—you can cover them up and hope nobody notices, or you can have a good laugh and share your misfortunes with your buddies in the hope that they'll avoid the same mistakes. And if you're really proud of your screw-ups, I guess you write a book about them.

The truth is, there are many specialists in today's world but few general handymen. And while nobody will fault you for not knowing how to power up a nuclear reactor or finding all the loopholes in your 1040, you'll be judged by a different standard when the car stalls, the house goes dark, or—God forbid—the keg quits working. It is here, on the shoulders of dark roads and the basements of old houses, that the tips in this book will become invaluable.

There are no all-knowing men. None. Not your mechanic nor your electrician, not even the old codger that lives down the road, eking out a living by repairing lawnmowers (well, he's probably pretty close). Sometimes, just being able to share your misery is the first step toward walking out of it. In these pages, you'll see that there are plenty of those mistakes to be made—I've gone ahead and explored a good majority of them. They might not be fun at the time but they sure are a learning experience. And they make for some interesting stories.

So lean back, crack open a beer, and we'll . . . what's that? No bottle opener? Hell no, don't put it back.

We'll get her open for you.

SECTION 1

General Automotive

Operating a Stick Shift

A stick, or standard, transmission, offers quite a few advantages over an automatic transmission. They get better gas mileage, allow you to operate at higher RPMs for extra power, and if driven correctly, will significantly extend the life of your brakes. Most importantly, though, they're just plain fun to drive.

But we've all seen it: a jerking, screeching car, usually piloted by an overanxious teen. The car lurches forward, brake lights flash, and the car stutters, shakes, and finally stalls. Bad enough for a socially conscious teen, but downright mortifying once you've moved into the smug ranks of adulthood.

The key to avoiding "dumping the clutch" requires remembering one very simple rule: *You're going to make a complete and utter ass of yourself the first few times you drive a stick shift.* No matter who you are, or what you drive, you're going to look like a moron. I'd lay ten to one every driver on the NASCAR circuit dumped the clutch on their first drive. Granted, some of them were probably only six years old at the time, but nobody has an untarnished record.

Once you've accepted this, you're free to find the "sweet spot" on your stick shift. This is simply the magical point where the clutch engages the transmission, when pressing the gas pedal actually makes the car go somewhere instead of just revving the engine. Finding this spot is the only difficult part about driving a stick shift.

The key is practice. A new BMW in the dealer's parking lot isn't exactly ideal; a hayfield or deserted parking lot, coupled with an older vehicle with a worn clutch, will make the initial stages much easier. Start with the car turned off and in gear, the most common situation for a parked car with manual transmission. Push the brake (middle) pedal in with your right foot, then depress the clutch (left pedal) all the way to the floor with your left foot. Once the clutch is fully depressed, the car will act like it's in neutral, hence the "brake-first" philosophy.

Start the engine with the clutch in and the vehicle in first gear. First gear is almost always all the way to the left and up. You may want to run through the gears before you start moving, keeping the clutch depressed at all times. Try slowly releasing foot pressure until you feel the RPMs fall off. The car may even shudder a little. Press the clutch back in, then repeat the process until you know exactly how far you can let the clutch out before it goes into this "pre-stall." That's it; that's the sweet spot, the point at which your right foot must make that brave journey from brake pedal to gas pedal.

So do it.

Press the gas (lightly!) just before the sweet spot, then let up on the rest of the clutch and add more gas as needed. If the car shudders and seems like it's going to stall, press in on the clutch, then slowly let it out again and apply a little more gas.

Assuming you haven't crashed into anything and haven't killed the motor, you should be rolling along. Now you'll need to either stop or shift up into the next gear. To stop, just push in the clutch and then the brake. To upshift, accelerate until the motor is revving a little higher than you'd normally hear in an automatic transmission. Take your foot off the gas, then press in the clutch and shift into the next highest gear (in this scenario it's second gear, you animal). Let out the clutch again and press down lightly on the gas. First gear is always the most difficult; subsequent shifts are a lot easier, since the car's momentum keeps the engine from stalling.

You'll quickly learn that a stick shift is a much more interactive vehicle than an automatic transmission, which of course is part of the fun. Listen to the motor to determine when to shift. If the engine revs too high, shift into a higher gear; if it acts sluggish, or seems like it might stall, downshift a gear.

If you need to stop suddenly, press in both the clutch and the brake at once. Pressing just the brake will stop the car, but it will also cause the car to stall. Gradual stops or slowdowns are best accomplished by working your way down through the gears, letting out the clutch at each gear. This allows the transmission to slow your car, saving wear on the braking system.

Leave the car in first gear when you park. If you leave the car in neutral, and don't apply the parking brake, it will roll on even the slightest incline. Leave it in first gear, and set the parking brake as an added precaution.

That's it. Give yourself a little bit of practice, then take that stick shift on the road and give it a try. If nothing else, rush hour traffic will be a lot more exciting.

 ## Roll-starting a Manual Transmission Car

A stalled manual transmission car with starting problems doesn't necessarily have to be jump-started or fixed on the spot. Unlike an automatic transmission vehicle, a stick shift can be roll-started. All you need is a little bit of juice in the battery, a clear stretch of road, and a little help.

Hook your car up to another car with a tow strap, turn on the key, and put the transmission in second gear. Leave the clutch in, and have the towing car pull you until you reach a speed that would normally be a little too high for second gear, then "pop the clutch," that is, let the clutch out at once. The car will jerk as the transmission is engaged, which should cause your engine to turn over and start. Make sure you push the clutch back in right away and apply gas. Lacking another vehicle, have a helper or two push you.

The target speed depends on the specific engine size and gear ratio of the stalled vehicle, but a general rule of thumb is a target speed of ten to twelve times the gear you're in. If you're going a *lot* faster than you normally would for the gear you're in (e.g., forty miles an hour and you pop the clutch in second gear) you're going to get one hell of a jolt, and might even ruin the transmission. It's always best to err on the low side. If the car sputters but doesn't start, just press the clutch in and try it again at a slightly higher speed.

Once it starts, press the clutch back in and signal to the vehicle pulling you to stop. Once it stops, move forward just enough to take slack out of the tow strap, and then put the car in neutral, set the parking brake, and disconnect the tow strap.

If you had a dead battery, be sure to keep the car running for at least ten minutes so the alternator can recharge the battery. If it wouldn't start because of a mechanical or electrical problem you'll need to get it fixed right away—or spend the rest of your life parking on hilltops.

3 Changing a Spare Tire

It was getting dark, and the railroad grade was utterly deserted. My girl-friend, who would later become my wife, was sitting in the passenger seat. It was a bumpy ride to begin with, but it got a lot worse when the front tire suddenly sprouted a railroad spike. I pulled onto the shoulder and killed the engine, then sat there watching the cloud of hungry mosquitoes on the other side of the windshield.

"Well," she said. "Under five minutes?"

"Maybe," I said. I drove in rough country then, and had gotten rather quick about my tire changes. But this was my dad's truck, on loan, and I wasn't sure where everything was. "Probably more like ten."

Hah. In the dark, finding and assembling the jack alone took at least twenty minutes. Simply releasing the spare tire, held tight to the frame under the body of the truck by some mechanism I still don't understand, took an hour. By the time I finally got everything together, I discovered the mechanics must have cranked up the air wrench the last time the tires were rotated; I nearly ripped a back muscle trying to loosen the lug nuts. When the most stubborn of the six finally let go it went all at once, sending my knuckles smashing into the rim.

Did I mention the mosquitoes? There was blood everywhere, all over my hand, running down my wrists and onto the tire iron. Should have been easy pickings for the little vampires. Obviously my eyelids were more tempting; I nearly smacked myself in the head with the tire iron when I tried to swat at one particularly persistent little bastard.

My future wife picked this moment to stick her head out the door. I could see the question on her lips—*What's taking so long?*—but she never actually asked it, just took a long look at me and then slowly retreated back inside the cab. Considering what I looked like, kneeling there with a tire iron gripped in one bloody fist, it probably seemed like the best option.

In some locations, there is no such thing as a cell phone signal. Those are the same places where it's usually many miles to the nearest service station. Faced with a long walk through dark and unfamiliar country, a few minutes kneeling in the dirt to change your own tire can seem like a downright bargain.

First, locate each component of your tire-changing system. Every car should have a jack, tire ratchet or iron, and a fully inflated spare tire. If the spare tire isn't someplace obvious, such as under the carpet in the trunk, it's probably held in place underneath the car by a cable. Obviously a dark railroad grade isn't the optimal place to locate these things; your driveway on a Sunday afternoon is a little easier.

Experiment with the ratchet and jack until you can tighten/loosen or lower/raise each one, respectively. Many times the ratchet also operates the jack—there's usually an instruction manual in the spare-tire or jack holder. The ratchet may come in two pieces, with a long "socket bar" that slides through the ratchet.

Mechanics often overtighten lug nuts to prevent liability issues, sometimes far past required levels. Since you've got everything out, pop off the hubcap and try to loosen one of the lug nuts. If it won't turn, try sliding a section of metal pipe over the end of the ratchet handle. This is called a cheater pipe, and the technique can be used on any wrench or ratchet to increase leverage. If the lug nut turns with the cheater pipe, be sure to stash the pipe somewhere in the car, preferably next to the jack.

If the lug nuts still won't turn, bring your car into the dealer or a mechanic and ask them to loosen the lug nuts to an acceptable pressure, somewhere around 150 foot-pounds of torque. The exact number should be in your owner's manual. Of course, you're better off too tight than too loose, but it's no good being stuck somewhere with a flat tire that you can't change, either.

Long spans between tire changes can basically weld lug nuts in place. A little penetrating oil—or in a pinch, a splash of cola—will usually loosen rusted lug nuts pretty quickly. Measure the pressure in your spare each time you check the other tires, since long periods of inactivity can bleed the air out. Having a can of inflatable tire sealant is always a good idea, although they make repairs more difficult at the tire shop.

Now that you know where everything is, understand how to operate the jack, and have a functional spare tire, go ahead and relax. You probably won't get a flat the rest of your life.

Use a length of pipe to increase leverage for stubborn lug nuts.

However, if you still manage to stick something pointy in one of your tires, make sure you find a safe, level place to change your tire. Hopefully this means a parking lot, but it's often the shoulder of the road. If this is the case, turn on your hazard lights and keep your feet out of the highway. Always turn off the engine and set the emergency brake.

Slide the jack under the axle or jack plate next to the flat tire, making certain it's seated firmly so it won't slip. Pry off the hubcap with the flat end of the socket bar or tire iron, and then use the ratchet to slightly loosen each of the lug nuts, but do not remove them. Then jack up the tire, remove the lug nuts (a hubcap works great to hold them), and slide the tire off. Put the spare on, and then start the thread on each lug nut with your fingers. Use the ratchet to tighten each lug nut until the tire starts to spin, then lower the jack for the final tightening.

You'll want to drive slowly at first, making sure there's no wobble in the tire. You'll get the hang of it in no time, especially if you practice first. Soon enough you'll be able to change a tire in five minutes.

Well . . . maybe ten.

 4 **Changing Brakes**

"Well," I said when my buddy sat down next to me, "how'd it go?"

He shook his head. "Not good."

We were in a sports bar, just about to watch the game, but when the waiter came over he ordered a glass of water. We were college-poor, but not quite at water-drinking levels yet. I knew then that it was a lot worse than *not good*. "How much they get you for?"

He sighed. "Six hundred."

I just about spit my beer out of my nose. "Six hundred bucks to change your brakes? Did he put in titanium-plated pads?"

Section 1: General Automotive

"I dunno," he said, sipping his water. "Maybe."

He didn't even know it was a joke. Not just my titanium quip, either—he didn't how much of a joke it was to pay somebody $600 for a job that usually takes a few hours and costs less than $100 in supplies.

Brakes last an average of about 20,000–40,000 miles, depending on how and where you drive. For some drivers, this can mean changing brakes as often as every year—an expensive proposition.

Car mechanics are, by and large, a good bunch of people, but they're out to make a buck like anybody else. They will overcharge you for anything even remotely complicated. The good news is changing brake pads isn't complicated, and it doesn't take much in the way of tools, either.

In almost every car and truck, disc brakes are now the norm. The design is simple—imagine holding up a bicycle and spinning the rear tire. You want the tire to stop, you press your thumb and forefinger on each side of the tire, using friction to stop the tire from spinning. With disc brakes, your thumb and finger are the pads (discs); the spinning bicycle tire is the rotor (a dinner plate–sized metal disc attached to the axle, just behind the actual car tire). Your hand is like the caliper, which holds the pads in place and squeezes the rotor.

In many vehicles, the front brakes bear the majority of the braking duties and are consequently the only ones that need to be replaced. Some newer vehicles have computerized mechanisms that distribute more braking power to the rear tires, in which case you'll probably have to replace all four sets.

Jack up the car and remove one of the front tires. You'll see the caliper perched on the top half of the rotor. Most calipers are held in place by two long bolts, usually with a star- or hex-indent head, located on the backside of the rotor. Loosen and remove the two bolts, then carefully remove the caliper from the rotor—it'll slide off. Don't twist the caliper or let it drop—the brake lines could break or crimp.

Check the rotor for grooves or wear; it should be smooth. If your car was shaking when you braked, you'll need new rotors no matter how they look: The shaking is caused by a warped rotor, which can be hard to spot. Simply remove the rotor—you may need to beat on the back side with a rubber mallet or piece of two-by-four. Worn rotors can be "turned," which means the metal is ground smooth by a mechanic. Or, you can simply replace the warped or grooved rotors with new ones. They slide right onto the hub. Be careful not to get any grease or dirt on the new (or repaired) rotors.

Next, remove the old pads (two per caliper, one for each side of the rotor) and snap in the new brake pads. Replace pads one at a time, using the other side as a template to make sure you put them in the right way. Use large pliers or channel locks to gently open up the inside of the calipers again—the pressure of the braking system tends to close up the pads when they're not pressing on the rotor. At this point you may have some brake fluid spill out onto the floor, so be sure to have a drain pan positioned under the brake fluid reservoir. Again, be careful not to get grease or oil on the pads. Slide the caliper back over the rotor.

Insert the two long bolts and retighten the caliper, then replace the tire and retighten it. You must replace brakes on both sides of the car in one sitting; replacing only one side can cause the braking system to fail. Once all the brakes are replaced, go for a slow test drive on a level road. If you hear metal scratching you probably put the brake pads on the wrong way (yup, I've done this). Just take the tire off and put them back in the right way—the metal tabs will score the rotor.

Pads and rotors can be bought at any auto supply store (pads are about $15 to $25 per tire, rotors about $25–$50 per tire). All you need to tell the clerk is the make and model of your vehicle, plus the year it was made. Time-wise, figure on spending an hour per tire, maybe twice that the first time you change them out.

That's it. After the test drive, go out and celebrate the hundreds of dollars you just saved. And save that glass of water for the morning after.

Fixing a Flat Tire

Tires come in two basic varieties: tubeless and, uh, tubed. Don't be overwhelmed by the technical language; the difference—and this is a shocker—is the presence of an inner tube.

An inner tube is a rubber bladder on the inside of the thick outer tire. Tires with inner tubes are most common in farm and utility vehicles, which tend to suffer more flats than street vehicles. Almost every car or truck tire is tubeless, as are wheelbarrow and riding lawnmower tires. Tubeless tires are generally tougher to fix yourself, but by no means impossible. If there's any doubt, look on the sidewall of your flat tire. The presence of an inner tube is clearly marked.

Patching Inner Tubes

You can patch inner tubes with a simple repair kit available at most auto part stores. Remove the valve core, a piece of threaded metal inside the valve stem (where you normally inflate the tire) with valve pliers; if there's any air left in the tire, it'll come rushing out all at once. Sometimes a pair of thin needle-nose pliers can be substituted for valve pliers.

Now slide the flat edge of a crowbar over the rim and under the inside edge of the tire—*not* the inner tube. If you pinch the inner tube you've just doubled your work, as they're flimsy and puncture easily. Push the crowbar down, which will open up a gap in the tire. Then, using either another crowbar or a large screwdriver, move down the arc of the rim and pry up another section of tire. Working a section at a time, move down far enough with the second crowbar so that the original one doesn't slide back over the rim. Once you reach the halfway point things get a lot easier.

Once the tire is off the rim, reach inside and slide the inner tube out. If you can't see the puncture, just add a little air to the inner tube, then mark the leaky hole with a marker or grease pencil. Really small holes can be located by pushing the inflated tube into a trough of water and looking for bubbles.

Sand the area around the puncture with a scuffing plate or sandpaper, then apply the patch from the repair kit and clamp it into place. Burn the rubber patch on, allow it to cool, and reinflate the tube to confirm the patch is working (you'll need to temporarily reinstall the valve core).

Getting the tire on and off the rim is usually the toughest part of any tire repair job. Work a section at a time, using one crowbar to hold the tire in place and the other to pry up another section of tire.

Deflate the inner tube, and then carefully slide it back inside the tire. Make sure you match up the valve stem with the hole in the rim.

Now, working in reverse, use the crowbars to pop the tire back underneath the rim, again being careful not to pinch your newly repaired inner tube. Once the tire is back over the edge of the rim, coat the edges with dish soap, then reinstall the valve stem and air it up. The tire will expand outward, then pop when it seals. The dish soap helps lubricate the rim, helping the tire slide up to form a bead.

Patching Tubeless Tires

Tubeless tires involve a slightly different approach. If the leak is coming from the sidewall—the side of the tire—then the tire is ruined. Large holes, caused by things such as railroad spikes, will also send your tire to the scrap heap, no matter where they are in the tire.

Simple nail holes are a whole 'nuther ball game. Rubber strip repair kits are worth their weight in gold, and they're available at most auto repair stores for under ten bucks. These kits come with plugs, plug holders, and a pilot hole driller. Pull out the offending nail, screw, or whatever caused your flat tire. Then use the pilot hole driller—basically a sharpened file—to ream out the hole. I sometimes use a cordless drill with a small bit to clean out the hole instead, since it can be tough to get the rubber plug inside smaller holes.

Thread a rubber plug onto the plug holder, push the plug in at least halfway (but never all the way), then twist the plug holder and pull it out. The plug should stick in the hole and form an airtight seal.

Plugs are meant to be temporary fixes. One of my temporary fixes lasted almost thirty thousand miles, but that's not commonplace. Regardless, these tire repair kits, coupled with a twelve-volt air compressor, can get you back on the road in minutes.

 Changing Oil and Air Filters

I have a confession to make. A deep and dark secret, the kind of thing no "real guy" should probably admit to. Ah hell, it ain't that bad—my wife changes my oil. Checks my air filter, too.

Of course, I've changed my oil and air filter many times, a simple task all guys should know how to do—as should their wives, girlfriends,

Drain Plug

The oil drain plug will be at the bottom corner of a telephone book–sized pan.

sisters, or anyone else they can talk into doing the dirty work for them. It's easy and cheap, and done regularly is about the best thing you can do to keep your car running smoothly.

You'll have to find out what kind of oil filter you need first. Ask an auto store clerk, or just look under the hood and jot down the number on the side of the oil filter (sometimes you'll need to crawl underneath the car to find the filter). The oil cap will indicate how much and what type of motor oil you'll need. In very cold climates, switching over to a five-weight oil (5W-30) in the winter makes good sense, since it's less viscous and reaches the pistons a little quicker on those frosty mornings.

Once you've got oil and a filter, the only other thing you need is a wrench, drain pan, and maybe an oil filter wrench. Slide underneath the car (use ramps if necessary) and locate the drain plug. This is usually about one-quarter to one-third of the way back from the front of the car, under the oil pan. The oil pan is metal, usually square with rounded edges, and the drain plug is simply a bolt head. Newer vehicles sometimes have a plastic shroud on the underside, which makes accessing your oil pan a bit more difficult.

Remove the drain plug and let the oil drain into a pan. If there's any doubt in your mind that this isn't the oil pan, just check the oil level after all the fluid has drained out. It should be mostly dry, with just traces of oil on the dipstick.

Next, locate the oil filter and twist it loose. If you can't do it by hand, use a filter wrench (a few bucks at any automotive store) or large channel locks. For really sticky filters, drive a screwdriver right through the oil filter and use the handle for leverage. More oil will flow out once the filter is loosened, so have the drain pan in position.

Rub some fresh oil along the rubber gasket on the new filter, then thread it on and hand tighten. Don't use a filter wrench to tighten it (or the screwdriver trick, for that matter). Unless you're very weak, hand tightening provides a perfect seal. Then thread the drain plug back into place and tighten it securely with the wrench.

Fill the car up with fresh oil, checking the dipstick occasionally so you don't overfill. Oil level should be within the two lines.

Start her up, keeping an eye on the oil pressure gauge and the temperature gauge. If either one moves into the red, or if you hear any funny noises coming from your engine, immediately shut off the car and check the oil again. Starting the car will pressurize your oil system, and much like turning on your water main after a plumbing repair, this is the time when you'll see if you have any leaks.

Odds are you won't. Check the oil again the next day, and again in a week to be sure everything is fine. The whole process takes about ten minutes and usually costs $10–$15. Any commercial oil-change place has to take your used oil at minimal or no charge. They won't advertise it, but it's the law. Just place your used oil in a sealable jug and drop it off. Most places will limit you to five quarts per visit.

Air filters are even easier to check and replace. There's usually a gauge on the outside of the air filter, a clear plastic cylinder that will say, roughly, "change when red." I don't really trust these gauges, and neither do many mechanics. Instead, open up the hood and unlatch the plastic compartment that houses the air filter, then remove the filter. Sometimes you'll find strange material inside the air filter housing, such as dog food, straw, and cigarette butts. It's not the neighbor playing tricks, just mice looking for somewhere warm to eat their Kibbles and Chunks in peace. Vacuum all this out, and then kick that fat housecat off the couch and shag him into the garage (a clogged air filter can cause serious problems and drastically reduce mileage; the odor of a cat is about the best mouse-repellent around).

Now, hold up your air filter and shine a flashlight through it. The amount of light coming through the filter is a good indication of how much air can get through. If you're still not sure if it needs replacement, bang the air filter lightly against the wall. If you see a dust cloud, the air filter is probably close to saturation and needs replacing. Just purchase a new one from an auto shop and slide it into the plastic housing. They cost about $10–$20.

 ## 7 Changing Spark Plugs

One of the easiest ways to increase both gas mileage and horsepower is to change spark plugs and wires every 50,000 miles or so. It's also one of the most neglected maintenance jobs. No doubt mass hypnosis and an oil company executive are involved somewhere in the mix.

Gapping refers to setting the distance between the electrode and the plate, which will determine the length of the spark. Plug ends tend to wear down over time, and are prone to carbon buildup. While you can clean and gap old plugs, for the best performance just replace the plugs with new ones. They're only a few bucks apiece, and if you've got significant mileage on your car the plugs are probably ready for retirement anyways.

Some new spark plugs come pregapped, while others are adjustable. Use a simple gapping tool for the adjustable plugs, making sure the setting matches up with the manufacturer's specifications.

The easiest way to check your spark plug wires' efficiency is to open up the hood at night, or in a dark garage, while the car is running. Bad wires will light up the motor like twinkling Christmas lights. This is spark that should be going to your cylinders, but since the rubber sleeves crack over time, the electrical current is now arcing onto the grounded motor block. This translates into wasted power, less power, and more gasoline bought at the pump each week.

You'll need one plug and one wire per cylinder. For almost every motor vehicle on the market this will be four, six, or eight. A couple of economy cars operate on three cylinders; trade this in for a real car while you're buying spark plugs. If you can't see some

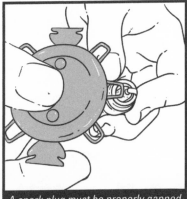

A spark plug must be properly gapped to work effectively.

of the plugs, you may have to remove parts of the intake manifold to get to them during the replacement (common in some V-6s). The key is to remove one plug and one wire at a time.

On older vehicles, spark plug wires lead from the spark plug to a central hub, called a distributor, which is supplied with central current via a coil. Newer vehicles may have independent coils for each cylinder. In either case, if you don't reconnect the wires in the proper sequence you'll affect the timing, which can have some pretty disastrous consequences. Think along the lines of those Indiana Jones movies, where Harrison Ford is weaving his way through a gallery of swinging axes and flame spurts, stopping and going at just the right time to avoid being killed. Now move old Indy forward a half-second in your mind's eye and you'll start to get the drift.

Timing, as they say, is everything.

Pull the wire off the plug, then use a deep-well socket (usually around a five-eighths-inch) to unthread the plug. It's important to have a deep-well versus the standard, shallower sockets, which won't reach down low enough to grip the sides of the spark plug. Remove the plug and hand-thread the new one into place. Apply final pressure carefully. If the plug is too loose, it could blow right off; too tight and you risk breaking it off. These aren't good things, so use a torque socket or wrench to be safe.

Once you're done, fire it up and listen to the motor with a fine ear. A choppy sound indicates one or more of the cylinders are "missing," that is, not firing. Go back and recheck all your wire connections, making sure to push down hard on the plug ends. It should give a soft "click" when it's fully engaged. If the problem persists, recheck your gap settings.

 ## Rotating Tires

"I need an alignment," I said.

"You do, huh?" the mechanic said, tucking a grease-soaked rag into his back pocket.

"Yup," I said, confident in my self-diagnosis. My truck had developed a noticeable shake and was pulling hard to the left, all telltale signs of a misaligned front end—or so I thought.

Twenty minutes later I had paid my fifty bucks and was on my way. I was two blocks down the road when my truck began pulling hard and shaking. I did a quick illegal U-turn and stomped back into the mechanic's office. "My truck's still pulling hard to the left."

He nodded. "Yeah, reckon it would."

"I just paid you fifty bucks to align the front end!"

I saw the barest glimmer of a smile. "And I did," he said slowly. "Didn't rotate the tires, though. They looked a titch uneven." The glimmer of a smile widened into a grin. "That'll cause your car to pull too, sonny."

The rest of the conversation wasn't exactly printable.

Tires do not wear evenly, especially in older vehicles, when ball joints begin to wear out, causing the tire to ride at a slight angle. There's no need to buy new tires just because one side is worn more than the other—you just need to rotate the positions of the tires so you have fresh rubber in the areas with the most road pressure.

Use a penny to check the depth of your treads. Slide the edge of the coin between the treads, head pointed down, and measure the amount of tread left on each side of the tire by using Abe's noggin as a reference. If you have sufficient but uneven tread—maybe his ears show on one side of the tire, and his chin on the other—then you'll want to rotate your tires. If Abe's entire head shows across the tire width, it's best to replace your tires, since they're too worn to provide proper traction.

Jack up one tire and remove it, then block the axle using a jackstand or big block of wood and move to the opposite corner of the vehicle. Remember to apply the emergency brake first, and always work on a level surface. The whole process takes less than an hour, extends the length of your tire's service, and often provides a smoother ride and even better gas mileage.

As a side note, excessive wear on the inside (middle) of the tire indicates a too-high air pressure; wear on both of the outside edges indicates underinflated tires. If your front tires have excessive wear on just one side, you may have worn front-end components, which can cause the tire to tilt and ride slightly on edge. You'll probably want to get a mechanic to fix those.

Just stay away from the ones that call you sonny.

Fixing Minor Dents

The light post never even saw it coming.

We were waiting in the parking lot for our fourth person on a double date when my friend decided a few figure eights would be a good way to pass the time. His specialty was a reverse doughnut, which to his credit he did quite well. Unfortunately for my friend—and his car—rearview mirrors don't work so well in the dark.

The impact certainly relieved our boredom. And it sure smashed hell out of the rear door. My friend was uncommonly quiet the rest of the night; no doubt thinking about the unwelcome prospect of telling his mother her car looked like it had met up with a good-sized moose. After the girls had gone home, we did our best to pull the dent out using a plunger. This sometimes works if the dent is smooth and shallow, but the plunger wouldn't even grip the side of the car. Next came the hair dryer, in the hope we could heat the metal enough that it would expand, pushing the dent outward. Eventually we gave up, because this wasn't a minor dent, and even if we had pulled out the depression the edges of the dent had crinkled. Crinkled edges won't smooth out, even if you can pull out the rest of the dent.

The easiest and most effective do-it-yourself approach for minor dents is to use an auto-body filler. Sand away the paint inside the dent and an inch or two around the perimeter, then fill in the dent with auto-body filler, which resembles putty. Allow it to dry, then sand it smooth and prime it. Most vehicles come with a small bottle of touch-up paint, which has your vehicle's paint number on it if you need to order more. Cover the primed area with several coats of paint, being sure to feather the edges for a natural appearance.

Both of the tricks we tried after our double date will work for less severe dents. In fact, minor pings caused by car doors or hail can frequently be cured with a hair dryer or just prolonged exposure to the sun, especially with dark-colored vehicles. For wide, shallow dents, try the plunger trick. Wet the end of the plunger to get better suction, then pull out steadily.

Some auto stores also sell pull-type repair kits, in which you drill a small hole, then insert a spreader through the hole, expand it, and pull the dent out via a connecting cable. You can then apply putty to the hole and paint it to match the rest of the vehicle. You can always remove interior components and try to bang out the dent with a rubber mallet, but with modern vehicles it seems like you have to dismantle half the car first.

10 Diagnosing Common Engine Problems—and Easy Fixes

No matter what else you do, there is an essential first step to diagnosing a stalled engine. First, open up the hood and stare down at the engine. Then frown and shake your head slowly. Finally—and this is important—say, in a disgusted tone of voice, "I *used* to understand these things, but *now*. . . ." Absolutely essential.

Truth is, new engines *are* a lot different than older models, especially since fuel injection and electronic ignition became the norm. Yet no matter how complicated they may seem, all gas-powered vehicles still operate on the same principles as Henry Ford's first Model T, and there are usually only three possible problems with a stalled or poorly running engine: spark, fuel, or air.

Before we dive into the engine stuff, first determine if you have a dead battery. If the car barely turns, or you hear a clicking noise (the solenoid) you may just need a simple jump start. You'll also want to check that both of your main battery cables are connected firmly to your battery and the negative has a firm ground. They can wiggle loose over time.

If you have battery power (the lights shine brightly, the radio still blares out Barry Manilow, etc.) but the car won't even turn over, you may have a bad solenoid or a stuck starter. If the lights dim and you hear clicking (the solenoid) when you try to start it, tap on the starter a few times with a hammer. Starters can seize up and often just need a little persuasion to engage the flywheel.

If there isn't clicking, and the lights don't dim, try jumping the solenoid. The solenoid, either a simple relay or a cylinder about half the size of a beer can, will have two or four metal bolts, or posts, sticking out or covered by a removable plastic cap. Use a screwdriver to bridge the solenoid post to the large positive post.

Make sure the key is "on" (full power to the accessories, without actually engaging the starter) and the car is in park or neutral. Jumping the solenoid provides electrical current to the starter, which turns the motor over. Use a rubber-handled screwdriver to jump the posts to avoid minor shocks—sparks will fly. Except for the lack of a handy

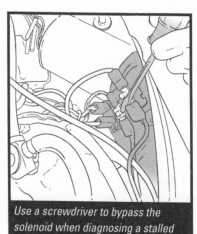

Use a screwdriver to bypass the solenoid when diagnosing a stalled engine.

remote control, this is also how those nifty remote car starters work. Solenoids can be on the starter, as shown, or situated somewhere along the firewall. Finding the solenoid is often the major challenge.

If the car turns over but still won't start, you've eliminated both a dead battery and a bad solenoid. This narrows the problem down to the same three elements needed for any fire: air, fuel, and spark. Of these three, air is the least likely to cause trouble. However, a disconnected vacuum hose can prevent the engine from starting, so look for any obviously disconnected hoses. A plugged air filter can also prevent a car from running.

Once you've eliminated air problems, check for spark. The easiest way to do this is to disconnect a spark plug, then reattach the plug wire and ground the plug to a bare metal surface. Either hold the plug against bare metal, or use a screwdriver as a bridge. Have a friend turn the engine over—you should see a spark jump between the electrode and the plate. If not, you've just diagnosed a spark problem. Leave the spark plug out for diagnostic purposes. And use those exact words if someone asks what you're doing.

One of the most common causes of a spark problem is moisture. If it's raining out, or if you just drove through a large mud puddle, or if someone just dumped a can of beer over your engine because you beat them in a race and won twenty bucks off them and their pansy-ass V-6, you'll want to check your distributor for moisture. This is the central hub for your spark (in older vehicles) and often collects moisture. Pop off the distributor cap and wipe it dry with your T-shirt (or that crisp new twenty-dollar bill), then try to start your engine. Newer vehicles probably won't have a distributor.

If you still don't have spark, try spraying a light oil lubricant, like WD-40, over the spark plug wires. This will displace any water inside the sheathing, and is sometimes all you need to get sufficient spark into your cylinders. If you still don't have spark, your coil(s) might be cracked and collecting moisture. Use a hair dryer to dry it out (newer vehicles might have a coil attached for each plug).

The most common fuel problems involve the fuel pump and filter. A clogged fuel filter is easily diagnosed, since it results in a gradual loss of power over time, and is easy to replace. Follow the fuel line forward from the gas tank until you see the filter, usually about the size of a soda can. Unscrew the fuel line on each end, then insert the new one and refasten it, making sure the arrow is pointed from the gas tank toward the engine. You'll get a little gas on your hands, so hold off on that celebratory smoke until you wash up.

A bad fuel pump is more likely to strand you someplace. While a bad fuel pump can be diagnosed by the presence of a jumpy or nonresponsive fuel gauge, or a long turnover before the engine starts, sometimes they quit working with no warning at all. To check if your fuel pump is working, turn the key forward, without actually starting the engine; you should hear a faint buzzing from the gas tank. If not, you might have a bad fuel pump. In all likelihood, you'll need a mechanic to replace it. This is the bad news.

Now, if your fuel pump goes out while you're driving, you're just plain-old shit out of luck. That's all there is to it. There's no easy fix, no way to get it started, just tow it to the mechanic and fork over the money. But to avoid tow-truck expense, pay attention to any shaking in your fuel gauge. Coupled with problems starting your vehicle beforehand, or significant mileage, it's a good sign your fuel pump is about to go out. Make an appointment with a mechanic before you get stranded somewhere.

The good news is a faulty fuel pump can sometimes be fixed, *but only if it quit working when the engine was off.* Fuel pumps can get stuck, locked into place as the components begin to break down, but you can often jar that old fuel pump into action one more time. The secret? Pound on the bottom of the gas tank. Bang on it with a hammer, piece of wood, or even your fist. While this might jar the fuel pump loose, it only works once. If it starts, drive it straight to the repair shop.

Still no luck? Much of your vehicle operates electronically, and all electrical functions are controlled by fuses. Many vehicles have two sets of fuses, one for smaller functions like windshield wipers and interior lighting (usually located in the interior, in the glove box or under the steering wheel) and another for heavier-duty stuff, like fuel pumps, which are usually located under the hood. It's worth a look; bad fuses will have a burned-out metal strip in the center. Replace any burned-out fuses with a less critical one until you can buy a new one.

11) Jump-starting a Car

A dead battery is about the most common mechanical problem you're likely to run into. Some manufacturers recommend avoiding jump-starting newer vehicles to avoid electrical surges that could damage the computer system. Done correctly, however, a jump start won't hurt anything.

First turn off all blowers, radios, lights—anything that requires power. This applies to both the dead and the "jumper" vehicle. Then connect the negative (black) cable from the negative post—marked with a minus (-) sign—on the dead vehicle to either the negative post, or the metal frame on the running vehicle. Then connect the positive (usually red or orange) cable from the positive post on the dead vehicle to the positive post (marked with a +) on the running vehicle. You'll hear a drop in the RPMs in the running vehicle once everything is connected properly.

Rev the engine on the jumper vehicle to increase the amount of amps flowing into the dead battery. If the battery was completely drained, you'll need to do this for a couple of minutes before the car will start. Larger-bore jumper cables work much faster than cheaper, thin-gauge jumper cables.

Disconnect the cables after the car starts, avoiding contact between the negative and positive clamps. While the resulting spark show is pretty cool, this could cause electrical problems to the vehicle still attached to the cables. Your call.

Some heavy equipment such as backhoes, dump trucks, and so on are positively grounded; others rely on two six-volt batteries. Connecting either via conventional methods described above causes all sorts of troubles. To avoid a smoke-and-light show, always trace the negative cable back from the battery. It should connect to the frame; if it leads toward the starter you've got a positive ground. If this is the case, simply switch cable order (only for the dead vehicle).

 ## 12 Pulling Someone Out of the Ditch

I still, to this day, have no idea how I survived this one.

An uncharacteristic January rain had fallen for almost a full day before changing over to snow. When the storm finally broke, we had about a foot of snow over a half-inch of ice, about the most treacherous driving conditions you can imagine. The couch and a warm fire sounded like a good spot to spend the day, but instead I found myself behind the wheel of the plow truck.

I cleared several driveways before I finally slid off into the ditch. Four-wheel drive didn't help—both my rear- and front-drive tires just spun on the ice. This wasn't something to get too upset about, since I was in my sister's driveway and her boyfriend's truck was sitting right there. He backed up his truck to mine, so our rear bumpers were separated by about ten feet, and we looped a chain around our respective ball hitches.

Should have been easy.

He took the slack out of the chain and tried pulling me out slowly, but his tires started spinning on the ice as soon as the chain came tight. Conventional wisdom called for "jerking it loose," that is, getting a run and yanking the stuck vehicle out with the other vehicle's momentum. He was on the second or third yank when I heard a faint pop of breaking glass. The next instant the lights went out, just blackness swimming in front of my eyes, and then I was sliding down onto the truck floor, all my motor control gone. Something small but heavy bounced across my lap, and I could hear, very faintly, the sound of safety glass tinkling into the rear seat.

I caught myself before I hit the floor, then madly began flexing toes and fingers. When those worked, I switched over to remembering my middle name and simple division; I knew what had happened, and figured I had to be either paralyzed or brain-damaged. But the toes moved, three times four was twelve, and I even remembered my Social Security number. Finally, convinced I'd avoided serious injuries (there are those that will argue about the brain-damage part), I sat up and looked around.

Directly behind me, at head level, was a baseball-sized hole in the back window. I looked down, saw a two-inch ball hitch lying on the seat, and put a hand to the back of my head. It came away sticky with blood. When I finally realized what had happened, I quickly scrambled out of the truck, convinced my legs and arms *couldn't* be working properly. After all, getting hit in the back of the head with a twelve-ounce piece of steel hurtling through the air on a flat trajectory is never a good thing.

I ended up with a headache and a broken rear window, and consider myself very, very lucky. Too many people are killed when chains snap, since even a single link can be fatal. In this case I'd been hit with the actual ball hitch, which my sister's boyfriend later admitted hadn't been screwed on tight. Come to think of it, I should have expected as much; he wasn't screwed on real tight himself.

The point here is that using a chain to pull someone out of the ditch is a recipe for disaster. There's just no give in a chain—they either work or they break, and when they break something goes flying. In my case it was a ball hitch, but many other times a length of broken chain will recoil sharply and connect with one or both of the drivers. On the other hand, a nylon tow strap will stretch, not break, and it's both lighter and easier to store than a chain. If they do break, they just slither harmlessly under the vehicle. I haven't used a chain since that incident, and never will again. Other than using a chain, though, the technique we used above was sound.

Attach the tow strap either to the frame, the receiving hitch, or the hooks under the front bumper of the stuck vehicle. You can also loop it around the axle if you absolutely have to, but avoid attaching a tow strap to a bumper. You'll just peel the bumper off, which is always entertaining but rarely effective. If you do this to a stranger's car just keep going—you can always disconnect the bumper a mile or so down the road.

Have the driver of the stuck vehicle straighten his wheels. Slowly take the slack out of the tow strap until it comes tight, at which point each driver should give a thumbs-up to signal he's ready. Try it slow and steady at first. If your tires spin, go ahead and try yanking the car out. Sometimes all it takes is a series of small jerks, other times you need to get a good running start and really yank it. You can bend or completely remove pieces of vehicle during this, so use your best judgment. Tow-trucks have a winch that can pull almost anything out, and it's not worth ruining your vehicle to save a few bucks. Make sure the driver knows to let off on the gas as soon as he's free; too often there's a collision when the stuck car pops loose.

If you're pushing someone out by hand, you'll probably have to rock the car out. Push it forward until the tires begin to spin (anywhere from a few inches to a few feet), then get out of the way and let the driver back up. You may have to push from the other end until it gets "stuck" again. Repeat the process, pushing the car as far forward as you can before the tires begin to spin, until you create a lane in the mud or snow. Ideally, this will provide enough room to build up momentum and break free of the ditch.

Getting Yourself Unstuck

Sometimes having four-wheel drive can be a mixed blessing. It's extremely useful for getting out of tough spots, but it also gets you into spots you have no right to be in the first place. And that, invariably, is when it quits working.

It was nearly dark and I was deep in the boonies. I can't remember what I was looking for, either a blueberry patch or a forgotten trout stream, but what I found instead were bait stations, piles of day-old doughnuts, and oats and molasses, left there by bear hunters in anticipation of the upcoming hunting season. Judging from the steaming piles all around me, old Yogi was a frequent visitor.

When I backed up to leave, my rear tire slid into a muddy depression and began to spin. Unfazed, I reached down and engaged my four-wheel drive. When I stepped on the gas the truck didn't move, and I heard a death rattle from the transfer case. I leaned my head on the steering wheel and groaned; my four-wheel drive, in the immortal words of some poetic hillbilly, had just shit the bed.

After a few minutes of tire spinning, I managed to sink down a few more inches into the soft ground and get myself truly stuck. Realizing the situation was hopeless, I reached down to call my brother-in-law for help—and then noticed my cell phone battery was dead. So there I was, stuck in the middle of a forest surrounded by bear food, with the sun already below the western hills, and nobody within five miles.

Bad stuff, man.

It turned out fine, of course. Few bears would trade a day-old apple fritter for sour Swede, and I made pretty good time legging it out of there, seeing bears in just about every shadow I jogged past. But it's easy to make it sound that way now, sitting here in a well-lighted room with two-by-six walls separating me from the wilderness just beyond my back yard. Looking back, I'm sure that younger version of myself wished he'd known a few things about getting unstuck with no help—and no four-wheel drive.

Don't spin your tires once it's obvious you're stuck; this is what psychologists call your denial phase. The only exception to this rule is if you have someone you don't care for standing behind you—a stuck vehicle can throw up an awesome amount of mud.

If you can move a little, creep in one direction until your tires begin to slip. Then stop, reverse directions, and go back until the tires spin again. Keep rocking the car back and forth, with the front tires straight, and try to extend the "stuck lane" until you can build up enough momentum to break free.

If you can't move at all, take out your car jack and raise the power tire (the one that's spinning). You may need to put something solid under the jack if you're in soft mud—a thick tree limb or even your spare tire works in a pinch. Once the tire is off the ground, put some roughage under it for traction. Evergreen boughs provide excellent traction and are fairly common, but regular sticks, or gravel from the shoulder of the road, will also work. You may want to line the rut you're in with branches or sticks so you don't get stuck as soon as you leave your original rut.

 How to Hook Up a Trailer

An older acquaintance of mine absolutely loved to fish. In fact, he was so anxious to get on the water that he often rushed off without double-checking his gear, and would frequently arrive at the lake minus some important piece of gear. On a trip to Canada many years ago, he forgot about the most important thing you can bring on a fishing trip.

Well, no, he did remember the beer. Second most important thing, then—his boat.

That's right. He traveled over a hundred miles in his truck (with a camper on back, blocking his rearview mirror) before he realized his trailer hitch had come loose and his boat had popped free on the highway, at sixty miles an hour, somewhere just past the Canadian border. I can't imagine the feeling he had when he pulled into camp, got out to stretch, and saw the empty space behind his truck. Knowing him, I *can* imagine the words that came out of his mouth. My ears ring just thinking about it.

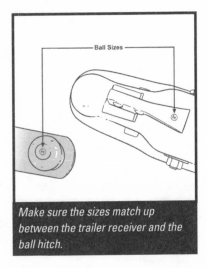

Make sure the sizes match up between the trailer receiver and the ball hitch.

Unbelievably, he found his boat and trailer sitting by the side of the road, unscathed, just a couple of hours later. He was pretty lucky, though (to qualify as *really* lucky he wouldn't have had any witnesses), because a trailer coming loose can cause serious injury to the trailer, its load, and anybody following you.

First, check to make sure you have the right size ball hitch for the trailer you're going to haul. Most hitches are made for 2-inch balls, but there are still quite a few $1^7/8$-inch ball hitches and receivers around. Look on top of the ball; there should be a size etched into the metal. There should also be a size etched into the top of the coupler handle. These *have* to match up.

Ideally, your ball hitch should be attached to a ball mount, which slides into a receiving hitch, which in turn is bolted right to the frame of your vehicle. Bumper-mounted ball hitches are too high for heavy loads, resulting in an angled trailer, and form a weak connection to the frame. If you plan on doing a lot of hauling, purchase a Class III receiving hitch and either get it installed or, better yet, do it yourself. It only

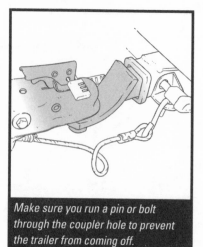

Make sure you run a pin or bolt through the coupler hole to prevent the trailer from coming off.

takes an hour and a little bit of elbow grease.

Now, slide the coupler down and over the ball. If it sticks, make sure the trailer is lined up straight. Then bring the coupler handle down, and slide a bolt or pin through the hole. Otherwise, all it takes is one good bump and the handle can pop up. One more bump and the coupler could bounce off the ball, and you're suddenly at a fishing camp without a boat.

Cross the safety chains for the best holding power. Attach them to the frame, not the bumper; most receiver hitches have a couple of holes to the side of the ball mount to attach the safety chains. Leave enough slack in the chains so you can make wide turns without them coming tight, yet not so much slack that the chains drag on the ground. As a final safety precaution, some trailers come equipped with an emergency brake, which is activated by a trip lever attached to a thin metal cable. Again, attach this cable somewhere to the frame. If both the trailer coupler and the safety chains come loose, the cable will engage the emergency brake and stop the trailer.

Now you need some lights. Simply slide the light adaptor for the trailer into the wiring harness from the truck. Sometimes this is flat and rectangular, commonly called a flat four. Flat fours have been largely replaced with circular, plug-style wiring connectors. If you have the wrong type of wiring connection, you can buy a conversion kit from the auto store and install it in a few minutes. The older type of connector is prone to corrosion, but a shot of WD-40 and a small wire brush can cure any contact issues in short order.

15 How to Back Up a Trailer

"Harvey!" the lady yelled, tugging on her scarf. "Harvey, they're *staring* at me!"

Fishing season had just opened, and I was waiting patiently to back my boat into the water. The woman hollering at her husband had just bypassed about twenty idling trucks, ignoring both common sense and common courtesy, and was now attempting to back her empty trailer into the water so her husband could load up their little sailboat.

It was a nice boat launch, with wide paved approaches and good lighting. Nonetheless, Mrs. Harvey had made about six different stabs with the trailer, alternating her jackknifes in a drill sergeant cadence: left, left, left-right-left. One time, much to the general amusement of the people she had bypassed, she ran one wheel up on the dock, leaving the boat tipped at a forty-five degree. It was at this time that she stepped out of the truck and beseeched her hubby for help.

Ole Harvey just shrugged his shoulders. He was holding the sailboat in place, and there was little he could say, except "Keep it straight" (to which I would have added, "And next time, wait your goddam turn"). Maybe he was embarrassed at her cutting in line, or maybe he just wasn't all that anxious to get in the truck with her. Either way, the meaning was clear: She was on her own.

After another five minutes or so she finally got the trailer in the water, and a few minutes after that they pulled away, red-faced, mouths working rapidly behind the windows of their truck. We watched them roll away the same way we'd watch a retreating storm, then quietly began to back our own boats into the water.

Hey, we've all been in Mrs. Harvey's shoes at one time or another. If she hadn't been so rude about cutting in line, no doubt one of us would have gone up to her and quickly revealed one of the easiest tricks in the

Position your hand at the six o'clock position, then simply move it in the direction you want the trailer to go.

world when it comes to backing up a trailer. And no, it isn't "Slide over so I can drive."

Straighten the truck and trailer so they're in line, then put your right hand on the bottom of the steering wheel, at the six o'clock position. Now *slowly* begin to back up. No trailer will move perfectly straight no matter how good you are; backing up a trailer involves constant minute adjustments that are best made at a slow speed. Looking in the rear- or side-view mirror, rotate your steering-wheel hand in the direction you want the trailer to go. If you want it to go left, bring the hand gripping the steering wheel up in that direction. If you want it to go right, swing your hand back in that direction. This one-handed approach eliminates the mental confusion associated with interpreting a reflected object, and allows you to sit comfortably, instead of twisting your body around.

If you're backing in an empty trailer and can't see the sides of the trailer, drop the tailgate of your pickup or open the rear door of your SUV. Again, just move slowly and make minor adjustments as you back up.

A few extra tips:

1. If you're backing a boat trailer into the water, be sure you disconnect the wiring before submerging the lights. Submerging your trailer lights is an easy way to blow out either a bulb or a fuse.
2. The shorter the trailer tongue, the tougher it is to back up the trailer. Go slower to make up for the lower margin of error.

3. Never leave your vehicle unattended while parked on the ramp. If you have to load the boat alone, set the emergency brake *and* use chocks under the tires. I nearly backed a friend's truck into a North Dakota lake because I forgot to do this.

4. If you're pulling a trailer and your automatic transmission keeps shifting, use the next lowest gear. There's no need to use third or second gear just because you're pulling a trailer; just make sure the transmission isn't being overtaxed by excessive shifting.

16 Riding a Motorcycle

My wife is always scared my motorcycle is going to get me killed. So far, the thing I've hurt the most has been my pride.

I've killed the engine at busy intersections, got hit with a rock in the very worst place a man can get hit with a hard flying object at sixty miles an hour (no, not in the eye), slid under a car and burned my leg so badly on the muffler that my skin turned into patches of greenish-purple bubbles, and wiped out at sixty miles an hour after getting unseated by a bird. Yeah, a bird. Motorcycles are dangerous, no doubt about it. Of course, they're also fun as all hell.

If you're familiar with driving a stick shift, you're well on your way to learning to drive a motorcycle. The main difference is that a motorcycle uses a hand-operated clutch and gas, with a foot-operated shifter. Braking is applied via both hand and foot, but only on the right side of the vehicle. Don't worry, it's not nearly as complicated as it sounds.

To start, you'll want the bike in neutral with the handbrake applied. Reach down and flip open the kickstart (or, if you want to be a pansy, use the electronic start). Once it fires up, press in the hand-clutch, and press the foot lever down. For most bikes, only the first gear is down, with the rest being up. You should hear a click as the foot lever pops up, which means you're in first gear. Let the hand clutch out, applying gas as you would for a stick shift. Continue shifting up on the foot lever until you reach top gear (usually fifth) and then downshift by pressing down on the clutch pedal until you reach neutral.

You can't steer a motorcycle by moving the handlebars, unless you're going under ten miles per hour. Instead, steering a bike is accomplished by leaning, exerting slight pressure on one side of the handlebars while shifting your body weight into the curve. Start out slow, making both wide and tight curves, before heading out onto the main roads. Be careful not to overcompensate, and don't take passengers right away, since they make steering much more difficult.

Unlike a car, the front and back brakes are separated. Many people brake almost exclusively with the rear brake, which makes steering during the slowdown easier, and also prevents the front tire from "plowing," or suddenly turning sideways and dumping you into the road. Hard braking with the rear tire, however, can cause the back tire to slide out from underneath you on loose gravel or wet roads. I generally apply about 75 percent braking to the rear and 25 percent to the front, but the exact ratio depends on road conditions and on the kind of bike you drive.

Your headlights should stay on all the time. Most accidents happen because motorcycles are tough to see and people pull out in front of them, so it's imperative you watch for inattentive drivers. Also watch for deer, dogs (they *love* to chase motorcycles, the mangy little bastards), and yes, even birds. Wear a helmet and shades. Bright clothing is recommended by most DOTs, so maybe this is your chance to break out that lime green, tie-dyed T-shirt.

The key is to practice at slow speeds, which are the safest if you happen to wipe out, and also the hardest to master. High speed steering is easy, as long as you don't overcompensate on a curve or hit something.

So go on out there and join the club, hop on your Indian or BSA, your vintage Harley . . . okay, okay, I've got an old Yamaha that leaks more oil than a bucket of Original Recipe. Really, it doesn't matter what you drive. Riding a bike is like being part of a gang, even if you don't bust up backcountry bars and chase pills with Jim Beam for breakfast. No matter what you drive, nine times out of ten you'll get a little left-handed wave from another biker when you meet on the road; if you run into trouble, the first guy there is probably going to roll to a stop on two wheels. We stick together, because when you get hit by a June bug in the lip at sixty miles an hour, everyone bleeds the same color. Well, except for the June bugs—they bleed a sort of yellowish-green.

Getting Out of a Speeding Ticket

"You know why I pulled you over?" the trooper asked, leaning down.

"I was going too fast." It was the second time I'd been pulled over in the last week. For all I knew, it could have been the same officer.

"You late to work?" he asked.

"A little," I conceded, glancing at the clock in the dash. "But no later than usual." I was a couple of miles away from my first cup of coffee, and a story just seemed like too much work.

"Know how fast you were going?"

"No idea," I said. "Maybe seventy? Seventy-five?"

He took my license and insurance information back to his cruiser while I sat there, wondering if he would bump the speed down into the lower-fine range. But when he returned he just handed me my papers back. "Just a warning this time," he said. "Keep it down."

"I will," I said. "Hey, thanks."

He nodded again, the brim of his hat covering his face for a second. When his mouth reappeared, his stoic trooper's face had cracked into what might have been a faint smile. "Quite a story you got there."

The average person gets pulled over maybe a half-a-dozen times in their entire driving career. It's a novel experience, if not a very pleasant one. We want to explain ourselves, to tell them the extenuating circumstances that make our situation unique. The average trooper, on the other hand, pulls over thousands of motorists every year, and they hear all kinds of stuff. *Nothing* is unique to them—unless it's the truth.

When you see the lights flashing behind you, pull over onto a safe spot. If you're on the freeway, pull as far over to the shoulder as you can, or better yet, find a *close* exit and get off the main highway. Once you're on the side of the road, put the car in park, roll down the window, and kill the engine. Then put your hands on the top of the steering wheel and leave them there. You can get your license and insurance dug out of the glove box later; at the moment, the trooper has no idea if you're an escaped convict rummaging for a weapon.

You've made the trooper feel safe and put him at ease. Now answer his questions truthfully. He knows damn well why he pulled you over, and so, in all likelihood, do you. If you have a fairly clean driving record and appear repentant, odds are he'll let you off with a warning. Of course, there's no guarantee. Sometimes they have a quota to make, and some situations all but demand a ticket. I was once pulled over at two-thirty in the morning going eighty miles per hour in my Camaro. Neither I, nor the trooper, said a word. I handed him my license, he went back to his car and handed me a ticket, and we both went on our way. We both just knew.

If you get nailed with a ticket you think is unjust, go ahead and meet the cop in court. If he doesn't show up, you win automatically, and this happens more than you might think. If he does show, ask about radar range and detection limits, interference, or any other situations you or Google believe could have caused an erroneous reading. Be polite, polished, and well prepared. The odds are excellent you'll walk away with a clean record—and your very first court victory.

How to Change a Serpentine Belt

I never realized just how many functions the serpentine belt controlled until one snapped as I was going down a steep hill. Suddenly I was without power steering, the voltmeter needle plunged downward, and the engine almost immediately started to overheat. Luckily, I got it home within a couple of minutes—and then spent the next seven hours trying to figure out how to get the new belt on.

The ideal place to change a serpentine belt is in the garage, before it breaks. Serpentine belts will start to crack over time, and a belt with more than ten cracks per inch is ready to break at any time. Go look; if there are over ten cracks per inch, at least get a new one and stick it under the seat—you're going to need one sooner or later. Still, it's always easier to change it at home.

There's usually a diagram right on top of the fan housing that shows you how to position the belt. If the belt is broken you can simply slide it out, but if you're replacing a functional

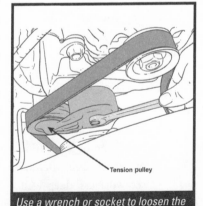

Tension pulley

Use a wrench or socket to loosen the tension pulley and release the belt pressure.

belt, you have to release the pressure on the tension pulley first. Use a breaker bar or long-handled wrench to move the tension pulley arm down, then slide the belt off.

Slide the old belt off the pulleys, then slip it around the front of the fan. Position the new belt over the fan and onto the other pulleys, using the diagram as a reference. Lower the tension pulley again, then slip the belt onto the tension pulley wheel. The belt has to be positioned with the grooved side down for proper traction.

Start the engine and listen for any whining or flapping, and check to make sure the fan and other belt-driven motors are turning. Keep an eye on your gauges, especially your temperature and voltmeter. If you replace an aging but functional belt, throw it under the back seat for a spare.

 ## Things Every Guy Should Have in His Vehicle

Outfitting your car with a few essential items will help you get out of a wide variety of jams, and should cost less than $100 total. They're well worth the small price paid and space used.

- 20'–30' tow strap
- Jumper cables
- Tire repair kit and a 12-volt air compressor
- Small can of WD-40 lubricant and/or penetrating oil
- Standard tools, including a crescent wrench, flathead and Philips screwdrivers, deep-well socket for spark plugs, and pliers
- A good, fully charged flashlight
- A space blanket, flares, first-aid kit, snacks, and bottled water

Section 1: General Automotive

- 1-gallon gas can, refilled annually and tightly sealed
- A CD containing both "Back in Black" and "You Shook Me All Night Long," by AC/DC; also, "The Gambler" and "The Coward of the County," by Kenny Rogers

SECTION 2

Disclaimer: The advice and suggestions below are written with the right-handed guy in mind. No disrespect to you southpaws; after all, it's a scientific fact that most people are born left-handed—the smart ones just overcame it.

 How to Hit a Straight Drive

Some folks are natural golfers. I'm a natural slicer, prone to big swings and what one friend refers to as "that unique flying elbow." Occasionally I try to play my splice by teeing up toward the woods, in the vague hope my ball will curve back onto the fairway. This is invariably when I hit my straightest drives, the ones where the balls scream out at a perfect trajectory, rising high off the ground until it thunks into a poplar tree a hundred yards out.

Inconsistency is undoubtedly the single biggest problem facing the average weekend golfer, and the only thing that can cure inconsistency is practice—lots and lots of practice. Since most of us just don't have the time to hit ten buckets of balls each week, we'll concentrate on some minor adjustments that can straighten out many of those errant drives.

Slices and hooks are caused by spin, which results from the clubface hitting the ball at an angle. Spin is inevitable, of course, but the key to straight drives is reducing *side*spin by presenting a straight clubface to the ball. Easier said than done, but there are a couple of tricks that can help significantly reduce the sidespin that causes slices and hooks.

First, try adjusting the height of the tee so you're only about a half-inch off the ground. Many people tee up much too high, which affects the point in your swing at which you make contact. Since the very bottom of your swing is the point at which the clubface is the most stable, simply pushing the tee down an extra half-inch to extend your arms a little more can drastically reduce sidespin.

Another old trick, passed on to me by my father-in-law, seems to work wonders for some people. Stick a handkerchief under the armpit closest to the pin, then simply make your swing without letting the handkerchief fall to the ground. Done correctly, this eliminates that flying elbow, presents a straighter clubface to the ball, and makes for straighter drives (and yeah, maybe a few funny looks).

Hit the ball toward the inside part of the clubface, which has less wiggle than the outside edge. Keep your eye on the ball, letting your momentum carry your head upward. Looking up before you hit the ball shifts your entire stance, which in turn shifts the clubface.

Lastly, and perhaps most importantly, try taking about 10 percent off the force of your swing. Any more than this and your grip tends to suffer, resulting in a floppy swing and weak, dribbling drives. But backing off 10 percent can work wonders, relaxing your muscles just enough to give a smooth yet still powerful swing.

Hey, odds are you aren't going to be making the next PGA tour even if you follow these little bits of advice. But you might stay on the green a few more times each round, and that's all most of us want anyways. If not, well . . . the woods *are* nice and shady on those hot summer days.

21 Getting Out of a Sand Trap

First, make sure nobody's looking. Usually this is right after someone who's a lot better than you bounces their ball onto the green. Then, while everyone's attention is diverted, grab your ball and throw it, quickly followed by a swing into the sand and a victorious whoop. You'll want to be consistent with your previous results; depending on how you're playing, you can either throw it onto the green or merely out of the trap. To keep everybody fooled, I usually throw mine into the woods.

A couple of less efficient but more ethical options involve the scoop and the plow techniques. Quite simply, you can either:

1. Try to pluck the ball out of the sand, assuming it isn't buried in the stuff and instead is just sitting there, looking like it's going to be the easiest shot you've had this whole miserable round, or
2. Hit just behind the ball, using the resulting explosion of sand to lift the ball up and out of the trap.

Both methods work. The scoop method involves a normal swing, but it requires a nearly perfect hit. Try moving back when addressing the ball, which means you'll catch the ball on your upswing and get better lift. A smooth follow-through and pinpoint accuracy are essential when using this technique, so take lots of practice swings.

The plow method seems simpler, yet is often more difficult for the average golfer. Basically, you're trying to create a small tidal wave of sand underneath the ball, which will lift it up and out of the trap. You'll have to hit the sand pretty hard to do this, and you need to hit right behind the ball—if you connect *with* the ball you're going to end up sailing way over the green and into the clubhouse. When this does work, however, the results are pretty neat.

I still opt for the hand toss.

 Hitting Out of the Rough

Swing like hell.

Actually, my preferred method involves using a half-dozen practice swings to clear out a lane just behind the ball, then use that path of beaten-down grass as an approach lane to my buried ball. Another nice method is to feign practice swings, all the while trying to hit the ball.

The trick here is to not act surprised when you actually hit the ball, and never make the mistake of wiggling the club head or—God forbid—staring down the pin. Just keep swinging, taking a small break to shuffle your feet between each swing. When the ball finally comes free, nonchalantly drop your iron back in the bag. Whatever else you do, do not look up to see your partners' expressions.

If you're one of those puritanical golf types, my first advice stands.

Open the clubface up slightly to hit out of the rough.

Swing like hell, and make sure you follow through to power through the thick stuff. You'll want to open up your clubface, as the grass tends to pull the clubface in when you drag it through the rough.

If you inch a little closer to the ball, you'll reduce the amount of grass you hit. This will also reduce backspin, so the ball will bounce longer than it might for a conventional fairway shot. The perfect shot out of the rough is going to be fairly flat, a roller more than a bouncer, so keep that in mind when selecting your club.

23 Greens Etiquette

It's amazing how hard it is for some people to stand still for more than five seconds at a time. Yeah, I'm talking to you, casual golfer. Think it doesn't matter? If LeBron James can make a free throw with 20,000 people screaming and stomping, your overpaid boss should be able to make a five-foot putt while you're shooting the breeze, right?

Well, yeah, he *should*. He also should have promoted you instead of Johnson. Hey, where is Johnson? Standing back at the edge of the green, not saying a word? What's he doing *there*?

Golf is a physically laid-back, relaxed game that requires moments of intense concentration. Not much different than your typical CEO or manager's day, actually. Of course, all kinds of people enjoy golf, from dog walkers to millionaire basketball players, but the mindset of serious golfers remains fairly constant. And it's not a state of mind that wants to be interfered with when the game is on the line.

Don't be the ball—be the golfer. Put yourself in their golf spikes, inside their patented leather golf gloves. You've remembered all those $100-an-hour lessons from the club pro, you've taken out a second mortgage to buy those oversized clubs that look more suited to clubbing badgers to death than hitting a three-ounce ball, you're at the tee box on Sunday morning and there's five bucks riding on each hole.

You tee up and, miracle of miracles, the drive goes straight and far. There's still a hundred yards to go, though, and you manage to wipe everything else out of your mind as you pull the iron out of the bag and separate from your foursome. Two practice swings, then you address the ball and everything is gone; next week's deadline, the dentist visit you've been putting off for two months in the hope the pain will just go away, the leaky sink—everything. Just you and the ball and the club, and there it goes, arcing into the air on a beautiful parabola, hitting the far side of the green and rolling to a rest not ten feet away from the pin.

Heaven, right? Well, depends on who you're playing with.

Time to seal the deal. At this point, concentration reaches a critical phase, with the focus centered on how the golf ball will "play"—how it will roll according to the terrain of the green. Whether you take golf seriously or not, this isn't the time for distractions. Even normally laid-back people get highly irritated with buffoonery at this point. And like all high-pressure situations, putting brings out the best and worst in people.

Listen, greens etiquette is simple. Just imagine you're playing for a hundred bucks a hole, and the guy putting is your partner. In other words, shut up and stand still until he's done. That's really all you need to remember. If you follow the rest of these simple rules, you'll be fine no matter who you golf with.

1. The guy farthest out goes first. If you're closer to the pin and your ball is even remotely in the way of the guy putting behind you, place a ball marker behind your ball (a coin is fine) and pick up your ball until he's putted past you. Then set the ball down in front of the marker, pick the marker up, and make your putt.

2. Never walk between another person's ball and the hole. This can leave a depression in the green, which can alter the course of a putted ball. Walk on the outside of the balls if you need to go someplace. Of course, never drive a mechanized cart on the green, and leave your golf bag outside the fringe.

3. Don't remove anything or alter the terrain in front of you in any way, shape, or form. This includes leaves, twigs, dead gophers, etc.

4. When someone is putting, you should not be on the other side of the hole, walking, talking, dialing a number on your cell phone, scratching your ass, or breathing heavily on the back of their neck. Just shut up and watch the clouds drift by for a few seconds.

5. If it's a long putt and the putter can't see the hole, offer to pull the flag. This means you stand next to the hole with one hand on the pole. Once the putter makes contact with the ball, pick up the flag and walk out of the way. Avoid the temptation to stop the ball with the side of your foot when it rolls past the hole. Even if the guy putting is your boss.

6. Put the flag back up for the next group. Nothing is more distracting than running down to put up the flag before your approach shot.

 Breaking In a Baseball Mitt

Unlike nearly every other piece of sporting equipment you buy, a baseball mitt is basically useless when it's brand new. The leather is stiff and hard, hardly ideal conditions for catching a wildly spinning ball traveling upward of 100 miles an hour. Before you even think of using your glove in anything more competitive than a pick-up game, you'll need to break it in.

There are two principles to breaking in a mitt: softening and forming. Rub in a light coat of oil or petroleum jelly, then place a softball into the webbing for a pocket mold. Some people use a baseball, but a softball provides a bigger pocket. Wrap the glove in extra-large rubber bands, then wind it tightly in an old towel, and shove it under your mattress, between the couch cushions, or anywhere with constant but shifting pressure. Leave it there for a week or two.

Then go play catch—lots and lots of catch. After a little while the glove should feel like it's grabbing the ball, snatching it out of the air like a Venus flytrap snaring a bug. You may want to add extra oil from time to time, but don't overdo it. Supersaturating your glove with oils makes it heavy and also causes the leather to break down too fast, resulting in a floppy glove.

 Throwing Breaking Balls

It was a few days before our first high school playoff game, and my turn in the pitching rotation was three starts away. Considering our playoff schedule, it didn't take a genius to figure out my pitching days were probably over. So, when our coach asked if I would mind tossing some batting practice, I was more than happy to comply.

There was a stiff wind blowing into my face as I situated myself on the mound. We had a fair array of hitters, one of whom would later be drafted by the Texas Rangers, and the coach told me to go ahead and do whatever it took to challenge them in preparation for the upcoming playoff game. My fastball was decent but not overpowering, so after a brief consult with my catcher we went to work.

And I started throwing junk.

With the strong headwind increasing the spin on my breaking balls, I threw strike after looping strike past my buddies. Sliders, curves, circle-changes—you name it, it was working. Occasionally I would throw a hard inside fastball, just to keep them honest, then follow it with a curve that started at their heads and ended up diving across the outside corner. They'd bail out, then get cussed out by our mercurial coach. I can't remember ever having more fun on the mound. I'm pretty sure I got some harder-than-usual towel slaps in the shower room later on, but it was worth it.

I ended up basically throwing a no-hitter in our batting practice. When the coach finally waved me over, I thought he might yell at me for having too much fun while our batters struggled. Instead of a reprimand, he asked me how my arm felt. When I said it was fine, he offered me the start in the playoff game.

By the time the game came around the wind was long gone and my stuff wasn't quite as good. We ended up losing that game by a run, but I struck out the side just before I was pulled, and only gave up a couple of earned runs. When I finally sat down, my ornery old coach said something about me being the type of guy you could rely on.

It doesn't mean much now. But those were the glory days, *my* glory days, and knowing how to throw a breaking ball was instrumental in playing my last game exactly how I wanted: up there on the mound, gazing over our dozen fans, hoping for the breeze to pick up.

No sooner had I learned how to throw a fastball in the general area of home plate than I was begging my dad to show me how to throw a curveball. To a young boy, a curveball is nothing short of magic, an act of some arcane technology reserved for big-jawed men on cool October evenings. Truth is, a lot of that mystique never does fade away.

Throwing a breaking ball is all about the spin. The same principles that send a golf ball slicing off into the woods also control the movement of a breaking ball. The more spin, the more break or movement your pitch will have. Basically, a spinning ball creates a lower pressure on the downward and/or outside edges of the ball, causing it to fall or curve outside of the straight line your throw should have warranted.

There are two basics to master when throwing a breaking ball: grip and release. How you hold the ball determines your release, which in turns determines the spin. There really doesn't need to be any excessive twisting or "chopping" motion during the delivery; a basic overhand throw with a couple of minor modifications can produce monstrous breaking balls. The grip and release for each common type of breaking ball is detailed below.

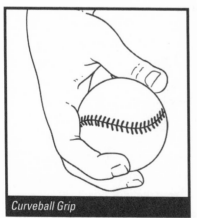
Curveball Grip

Curveball

For a curveball, typically defined as a pitch that dives vertically, the best grip is along the seam, with the bottom of the "horseshoe" nestled against your palm.

You can tuck your index finger in for a knuckle-curve, which is a highly effective and easily mastered version of the standard curveball. Keep your index fingernail trimmed short for the best fingernail grip. It's a good pitch, and woefully underutilized in high school and college ranks.

For both the standard and knuckle-curve, your thumb moves up as you release the ball, while your index and middle finger rotate down. Bring your hand down sharply and across your body, to the opposite hip (as opposed to the opposite *knee* with a fastball) to increase spin.

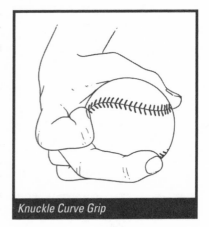
Knuckle Curve Grip

Change-ups

Circle or "okay" change-ups sound boring, but they can be downright deadly in conjunction with a decent fastball. The key is to throw with exactly the same arm motion, while subtly changing the grip of the ball to slow it down. Since most batters rely on timing as well as reflexes to connect with a pitch, this often causes a hitch in the batter's swing.

Grip the ball by making an OK gesture with your hand and overlapping the thumb slightly. Throw it exactly the same as you would a fastball, but rotate your thumb slightly down, so it's in the six o'clock position when you release the ball.

Circle Change-up Grip

Slider

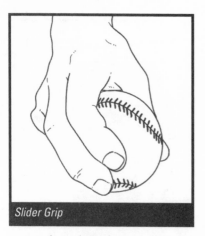

Slider Grip

A slider is a tough pitch to master for beginners, but an absolute bitch-kitty to hit once you've got it down. Hold it along the seam as shown, gripping the baseball on the outer third. Your wrist should be cocked slightly inward, but not stiff. The ball should roll off of the inside of your index finger on release.

My hands were never big enough to throw a split finger, but it's a darn good pitch to have in your arsenal. If you've got big paws, just press the ball as deep as you can into the webbing between your index and middle fingers, resting your thumb on the back seam of the ball. Then throw it as you would a regular fastball.

All breaking balls can be tough on the arm, as there's a lot of inherent twisting with the above grip and release. If you're thinking about teaching a youngster how to throw breakers, make sure his or her arm is fully developed to prevent injury.

 ## Batter Up: Tips for a Smooth and Powerful Swing

There's a great line in the alien movie *Signs*, where Joaquin Phoenix's character, a former minor league leader in both home runs and strikeouts, mumbles, "It just felt wrong not to swing." From Little League on, I knew exactly how his character felt. For me, the most dreaded thing on the baseball diamond wasn't the rocket-armed pitcher or those goofy lefties with their ass-backward breaking balls; it was that damn "take" sign flashed by the third base coach.

Despite usually batting cleanup for my baseball and softball teams, I was never disciplined enough to consider myself a good hitter. In fact, in one memorable game I actually jumped in the air to hit a particularly tasty-looking fastball. While you can't hit the ball if you don't swing, swinging the wrong way is worse than letting the bat sit on your shoulder. That's what they say, anyways—I really wouldn't know.

I do know some of the longest, sweetest balls I've ever hit were in deep fields where the fence was out of reach, or in softball tournaments where home runs were an automatic out. Instead of trying for the fences I swung naturally, smoothly, and the result was an efficient transfer of body mass into that quarter-sized area where bat meets ball. And those are the two keys to a powerful, accurate swing: smoothness and control.

A powerful swing has very little to do with big biceps. Arms and hands are simply vehicles for transferring your body's mass and energy into the ball. A good swing involves full body movement, not necessarily raw strength.

As the pitch is delivered, your body weight should shift back, much like a snake getting ready to strike. As you bring the bat forward, move your front foot toward the corner of the plate where the ball will cross. So if it's an outside pitch, your front foot should come down toward first base. Trying to pull an outside pitch leads to weak ground balls, while stepping into them can produce scorching line drives over the right-fielder's daisy-picking head. For an inside pitch, your front foot goes away from the plate, toward third base. Swivel your hips as you swing, keeping your chin tucked into your shoulder.

The difference between hitting a routine ground ball to short and a towering home run over the left-center wall is a matter of hitting the ball three-quarters of an inch higher or lower. With an uppercut swing (starts low, ends up high) the chances of hitting the ball squarely are much worse, since the ball and bat have a much smaller chance of being in the same place at the same time. A level swing also equates to a smooth swing, which in turn means more power.

None of this matters a bit if you don't have good hand-eye coordination. While some hand-eye coordination is undoubtedly inherited, don't believe for a second that what you got is all you can have. Playing stickball, lots of batting cage practice—hell, even hitting rocks with a stick will vastly improve your hand-eye coordination, turning those foul tips and weak grounders into line drives.

27 Judging a Fly Ball: How to Not Look Like an Idiot

It was a cold and wet spring day, one of my first games on the varsity team. The other two outfielders were seniors, one of them an All-Conference centerfielder, and I was trying desperately to prove I, a sophomore, deserved the left outfielder position.

It was a close game, and early in the fourth or fifth inning the opposing team's batter lofted a fly ball somewhere into the mid-atmosphere. I took a couple of quick steps forward, thinking it was going to be a shallow pop fly. Then, watching the ball arc over my head, I realized it was a lot deeper than I had originally thought.

I started to run back, my head turned over my right shoulder. But like so many balls hit into left field, this one was curving to the foul line. I snapped my head around over my left shoulder, trying to find the ball again. There it was—now I was *overrunning* it. I stopped, ran forward a few feet, and slipped and fell on my ass on the muddy ground. The ball landed a few feet away, almost exactly between the two muddy ruts my spikes had grooved in the field over the course of the previous innings.

I had run about twenty feet and all I would have had to do was stick my glove out. The coach was not impressed with my left field pirouetting—one of my teammates later said he had been laughing and then his face suddenly got red and he started swearing. I don't know about the laughing, but when I got back to the dugout I could certainly attest to the swearing.

My first mistake, and my most crucial one, was taking those first steps forward. Your first two steps should always be backward, and you need to have a little patience, especially with high fly balls. Some people have a natural ability to judge fly balls and can get a good jump on them, but they're probably not reading this section anyways.

Those two quick steps backward give you perspective, and even if the ball is hit in front of you it's *always* easier to go forward, rather than backward. But by backing up and moving with the ball, your brain can compute depth and trajectory much more easily.

Try to get behind the ball. If it's hit directly behind you, curve slightly to the right to keep the ball in sight easier—nothing can be quite so disorienting as a ball that's directly overhead. If you can, get a couple of steps behind the ball before it comes down, and then move forward as you catch the ball. This will help get your momentum going for the throw in to the cutoff man.

Softballs don't generally produce fly balls with the amount of spin and consequent curve as a hardball, but there's usually a lot more of them. Of course, nothing can beat shagging lots of fly balls before game time. And even if the baseball gods hate you and you end up with a towering, curving fly ball on a windy day during a close game, you'll probably learn a few new curses from your coach and teammates.

So you got that going for you, anyways.

28 Throwing a Spiral

Nothing says pansy like a poorly thrown football. Sad but true, and even big hulking guys—hell, *especially* big hulking guys—throw those ugly wounded ducks up for all the world to see. I cringe just thinking about it; it's almost like watching that full-grown man run away screaming when he sees a mouse—something you just don't expect, nor want, to see.

Just like throwing a breaking ball, throwing a spiral is all about grip and release. The tips of your fingers should be just over the top of the lacings. Grip the ball as far back as possible without sacrificing a secure hold. Big hands make for nice spirals, since people with a bigger grip can hold the ball farther back without it slipping. Apply pressure mainly toward the back, on your thumb, index, and middle fingers. It may help to cock your wrist out a little bit.

Your hips should be in line with your target. Bring the ball straight over your shoulder, opening up your hips as your arm moves forward.

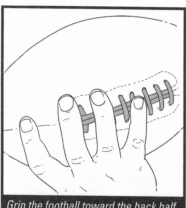
Grip the football toward the back half, with your fingers just over the laces.

While a sidearm delivery often produces nice spirals, the straight overhand throw is much more accurate and will actually clear the linemen's heads. It also lets you use your body mass to increase throwing strength.

The ball should roll up and off your hand, away from your thumb. It's important to leave your wrist a little limp when you release, which allows the ball to roll into a spiral.

Take a step or two forward right before you throw to increase velocity.

Except for certain Cheesehead quarterbacks, it's nearly impossible to throw across your body with any degree of power or accuracy. That's why a running quarterback will rarely throw to his non-throwing shoulder side—the body delivers most of the speed behind the throw. Arm strength alone rarely gets it done.

29 Punting

The trick to a long punt is the same as throwing a long pass—the spiral.

When punting a football, the ball should make contact with the top of your foot, behind the toes and slightly to the outside edge. This means you need to hit the ball with a solid but glancing blow, which produces spin. Much like a thrown football, a spiral improves both velocity and accuracy.

Catch the snap, then take three steps forward, starting with your right foot. The left foot is then your plant foot, and the third step will actually become your kick. Hold the ball straight out at chest level, pointed end out, and bring your foot up to it. You don't want to drop the ball. Instead, set the ball on top of your foot as it comes up.

The laces should be up, and you should hit the ball on one of the seams for the best spiral. Follow-through is extremely important and will increase the distance dramatically. Most professional kicking coaches recommend ending your kick with your toes at eye

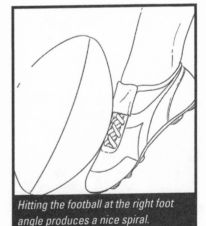

Hitting the football at the right foot angle produces a nice spiral.

level. I think the only time I accomplish that position is lying in bed, but you might be a little more flexible. Regardless of your limberness, a few stretches are pretty much mandatory before punting.

30 Tackling: Hitting Someone Like You Mean It

Seventh grade, a cold and rainy Monday afternoon.

I had strapped on shoulder pads for the first time a half-hour ago, and the time had come for our first full-contact drill. Our red-shirted QB was throwing little flat passes to receivers, with two men on defensive coverage. Everyone alternated between offense and defense, us pudgy seventh graders playing alongside husky ninth graders, some of whom looked like they shaved regularly after lunch.

I lined up in the receiver slot, ran a quick ten and out, and caught my first real pass. I enjoyed the sensation for about a quarter of a second, and then all the snot exploded out of my nose as one of those monstrous ninth graders pile-drived me into the hard ground. I had the brief sensation of my soul separating from my corporeal body, and then everything snapped back together like a rubber band. Everything, that is, except the snot dribbling down my chin.

"Welcome to football, you little punk," my tackler said.

I got up right away—you *always* get up right away—and trotted over to where the cheerleaders were practicing. By the time I got my bearings and rejoined the squad it was time for defense. Karma generally sucks for seventh grade kids, and this practice was no exception; the receiver I was about to defend was the same guy who'd ruptured most of my major organs a scant forty-five seconds before.

He grinned at me behind his beard.

I blew a snot bubble back defiantly.

Game time.

He caught the pass moving away from me, and the other defender hit him first. Well, "hit" is being generous; he sorta grabbed onto him and hung on. He slid down the receiver's leg, finally latching onto a shoe. Ole Beardface just stood there, trying to shake him off like a fox caught in a leghold trap. I was about five yards away.

I ran forward, lowered my shoulders . . . and hesitated. Just for a split second, but yeah, I hesitated. After all, he was a teammate, not an opposing player, and helpless to boot. What if I hurt him? By this time the coach had sensed my hesitation and was roaring at me to tackle the damn guy already, so I closed the remaining distance and piled my shoulder into his hips. It was like tackling a cement pylon.

I slid down his legs and fell on top of the other seventh-grader, still hanging desperately on to Beardface's shoe. My classmate grunted when I landed on him, then finally released his rigor mortis–like hold on Beardface's shoelace. Thus freed, Beardface trotted away disdainfully while I lay there on the ground, wondering if the cheerleaders needed a base guy for their pyramid.

I knew a guy perfect for the job.

I learned my first and most important lesson in hitting someone on the gridiron that day: *Never freaking hesitate.*

You aren't going to injure someone badly by making a clean, hard tackle. You may hurt them, yes. You may knock the wind out of them and raise nasty bruises on their body; you may sprain ligaments or even break a nonessential bone. You may even get a little boo-boo yourself. Usually, though, the only real physical consequence of a hard hit is that explosion of snot.

To tackle someone correctly, to hit him hard and clean, you have to keep moving your feet until you hit the ground. Hopefully the ball carrier is lying there with you, but it doesn't always work out that way. But if you run through the person carrying the ball, if you don't hesitate both before and after contact, you'll barely even feel the impact. Hesitate, though, and suddenly all the momentum is on the ball carrier's side, and mass plus speed *always* wins over mass plus hesitation.

The correct tackling form is simple. Shoulders should be down, roughly parallel with the ground, arms spread wide open, ready to grab and then wrap up your opponent after you make contact with your shoulder pads. Keep your chin up to see where the ball carrier is going. Ideally, your right shoulder pad should hit the guy with the ball in the waist, since trying to tackle shoulders or feet will often leave you with nothing but an armful of air.

Just keep your feet moving. Remember this if nothing else, because the guy you're tackling sure as hell isn't going to stop just because you touched him. Drive him backward, wrapping your arms around his body as you go. At the very least you'll push him sideways or at an angle, and if you hang on tight, help will soon be on the way.

(31) The Perfect Jump Shot

The following is a transcript from one of my high school basketball games, paraphrased from the local radio station.

. . . . *Swenson brings the ball up the court. He throws it to Johnson on the left side. Johnson looks in, quick pass back out to Swenson. Swenson swings it to the other side. Paulson has the ball, looking for Ostrander. Paulson drives, shoots. Off the rim, Anderson has the offensive rebound, just inside the free throw line. Anderson spins, shoots . . .*

Oohhh, now that was *an ugly-looking shot.*

Well, I was *rushed*, surrounded by defenders who were both taller and better jumpers than me. I had only a split second to turn, judge distance, and shoot. Typical game conditions, in other words. Even in pick-up games, opportunities for wide-open, unhurried shots are rare. Practicing these leisurely shots, then, doesn't make much sense.

To shoot well in a game, you need to practice game-type shots. That means jumping as high as you can while maintaining some semblance of form and accuracy; it means dribbling with your back to the hoop and quickly spinning to address the rim and shoot. Time after time after time.

For a right-handed shooter, the left hand is a guide. Position your palm flat along the left side of the ball. Rest the fingertips of your right hand across the lacing, so your fingertips are nestled in a groove. Push forward with your right hand, angle your wrist back, then snap it forward so the ball rolls off the end of your fingers. Never push the ball straight out using your palm, no matter how hurried you are. It's ugly and inaccurate—just ask my radio audience.

It's essential that your right elbow is tucked in, not cocked out to the side. You might even try aiming with your elbow—it can drastically improve accuracy if you normally shoot with a cocked elbow. In fact, keep *everything* in a straight line, from your toes to the tips of your outstretched fingers. If you develop a shooting style that's in-line and smooth, all you have to do is square up to the rim and judge distance. That's still quite a bit to do with a face full of defender, but it does eliminate the errors inherent with unorthodox deliveries.

A lot of your shooting range comes from your legs, not your arms. If you doubt this, stand on the three-point line and try to sink a basket without moving your feet. Since you rely on the power of your legs to power much of your shot, it's important to practice while jumping at game-level height, as mentioned earlier. Some people even put up a stepladder or other obstacle to shoot over.

Keep the ball at chest level when you start your shot. This gives you a quicker release and gets the ball up and away from the defender much faster. Release the ball at the apex of your jump, being sure to follow through with your wrist to create that all-important spin off your fingertips.

 ## Keeping Score in Bowling

With the advent of electronic scorecards, the simple act of calculating your own bowling score is becoming a lost art. But in order to truly understand how spares and strikes affect your final score, it's imperative you understand the basic methodology behind scoring frames. Otherwise you're playing blind.

You get two chances at each set of pins. If you knock down all the pins with your first ball, that strike, marked by an X, means you can add the next two ball totals to that score of ten. So, if you get two more strikes, your first box score will be a thirty. A spare means that you use both balls to knock down ten pins. Even if you throw a gutter ball the first time and knock down all ten pins with your second ball, it's still considered a spare. If you bowl a spare, add the next ball's total to that score.

In essence, throwing a spare or strike means you can double or triple your actual score. A perfect run of strikes equals a 300 score (the tenth frame actually allows you to throw three balls, since throwing a strike in the tenth score box means you need two more ball totals to calculate the final score; if you don't get a strike or a spare, you don't get to throw the third ball in the last frame). Throwing spares consistently, along with a couple of strikes, should land you in the 150–200 score range.

Bowling Accurately

It was Valentine's Day, and being the romantic fool that I am, I escorted my future wife to the bowling alley. Yeah, there's nothing like the smell of tap beer and communal shoes to really warm the heart of your girl on a cold February day.

My brother-in-law AJ watched me warm up, arms crossed, an expression closely resembling pity etched on his face. Finally he approached and pointed to the small arrows a few feet in front of the throw line. "Concentrate on those," he told me. "Don't even look at the pins."

"Yeah?"

"Sure," he said. "They match up with the pins. That center arrow is in line with the lead pin. The other ones correspond with side pins. Aim somewhere between the middle dot and the one alongside it."

Suddenly, as though someone had flipped a switch, I could bowl. Spares and strikes piled up on my scorecard, escalating my scores into unheard-of ranges (triple digits!). I quickly learned to throw the ball slightly off center, hitting between the lead pin and the number-three pin behind it. I didn't throw hooks, or throw hard. I just threw straight balls, at a medium strength, concentrating on the little arrows. And man oh man, how the pins fell down.

This is easy, I remember thinking as I tallied up my score, somewhere in the 220 range. Visions of 300 games raced through my head; with a little luck, I could be wearing plaid pants and carrying around a PBA card come next Valentine's Day.

As it turns out, that game was a fluke—I haven't come close to that score since. But my game has gotten a lot better, and even throwing straight balls I can still manage a respectable score most nights. And almost all of that is because I quit looking at the pins and started looking at the arrows.

Of course, using the arrows (or dots) as a reference won't help if the ball isn't thrown on a straight line from your hand. Start out by holding the ball in both hands, slightly to the left of the arrow you have your eye on. Keep your arm loose, which allows the weight of the ball to keep your delivery arm straight. When you bring the ball forward your arm should swing loosely, like a pendulum.

Unless you're a hard-core bowler, consistent strikes are tough with a straight ball. Better to concentrate on hitting spares as often as you can and let the strikes fall when they want to. To get a good number of spares, you'll need to consistently knock down seven or more pins with your first ball.

A three-step approach will usually build up enough momentum for consistently high pin knockdowns. Start with your right foot forward; this is simply a momentum builder and can be extended back two steps if you want a five-step approach. There are lines of dots behind the foul line to show starting points for both approaches; take a couple of practice strides before you actually throw the ball. Open up your hips to let the ball pass on a straight line. The ball should leave your hand just before it makes contact with the alley. Make sure you keep your wrist straight.

Don't even look up when you release the ball; instead, see if the ball crosses the arrow you aimed for. If it crosses the correct arrow, and the ball still doesn't strike the pins where it should, there's a hitch in your delivery. Try using a heavier ball; the weight keeps your arm straighter.

Oh, and one more thing. If you find a girl who doesn't mind greasy pizza and cheap beer on Valentine's Day, marry her. Besides the obvious good character traits inherent with such women, they're also a pretty inexpensive date for years to come.

Throwing a Hook

The reason professional bowlers maintain such a high average is simple: They use a hook ball to consistently score strikes. Scientific studies have shown that an angling ball will produce more knockdown power than a straight ball, even when they hit the exact same spot, but all the proof you need is right there on the PBA tour. It's hard to argue with a guy who considers eight strikes per game a dismal failure.

So why doesn't everybody throw a hook? Well, it can take some time to learn. Professional bowlers split their time three ways: drinking tap beer, searching the Sunday ads for polyester slack sales, and practicing their hooks (I'm kidding, of course—polyester slacks are *always* on sale). They've taken years to master what looks like a very simple technique. And at its heart, throwing a hook isn't terribly difficult. Throwing a hook *accurately* is where the years of practice come in, for which there is no easy shortcut. Still, you should be able to throw a hook, even if it's just because it looks cool.

Nearly all league and professional bowlers use a special resin ball that produces more spin. Much like a curveball, more spin equals more movement. If you're going to use a house ball, it's usually best to stick with a light one. It takes considerable wrist strength to throw a big hook, and even powerful men who aren't regular bowlers have difficulty getting enough twist on heavy, non-resin balls.

The thumb goes in the hole, but the rest of your fingers cradle the ball from underneath. Don't tuck your pinkie in, as this affects control and lessens spin. The motion on release is exactly the same as if you're throwing a football in an underhanded spiral. Your thumb, pointed up at one o'clock, should rotate to ten or eleven o'clock on release. Your palm should end up like you're about to shake someone's hand. Throw at a *slight* angle toward the right gutter; the ball should reverse movement about halfway down the alley.

Lanes are oiled to prevent damage, and this oil moves over the course of the game, spreading and thinning in some areas, piling up in others. Sometimes only the middle area is oiled, leaving the outer lanes dry. This means that each lane you play may affect the hook of your ball, so you'll need to adjust your technique according to the conditions of each bowling lane.

Picking Out a Cue Stick

When it comes to pool cues, most people who take the game seriously use their own stick. Most of the rest of us, who play occasionally at the bar or in someone else's basement, rely on a house cue. Approximately 99.8 percent of all house cues are as warped as your standard Jerry Springer guest, and a warped cue equals missed shots. The trick is to find the best of a bad lot.

To determine warp, lay the cue flat on the table and give it a little roll. Warped sticks will bounce and thump along the felt. Straight cues will roll smoothly.

Now rub your finger over the tip. Smooth, hard tips don't produce much in the way of spin, or English. There are abrasion pads made specifically for roughing up cue tips; they resemble a chalk box with an interior that feels like coarse sandpaper. If you can't find a "scuffer," you can try to use a file or some other rough surface to soften up the tip. A soft, well-chalked tip will drastically reduce those glancing shots that are the hallmark of the amateur billiards player.

Most cues will have a number written on the side, about halfway down. This is the weight of the cue in ounces, and typically ranges from the teens into the low twenties. I've always felt that heavier cues, around twenty ounces, give a smoother delivery. Some people use a heavier stick for breaking, then use a lighter one for the remainder of the game.

Once you've got the stick picked out, apply chalk to the tip about every other shot. Many bars will also have a cone of white chalk for your hands, which helps reduce friction on your guide hand. Keep your drink in your power hand, since condensation on your guide hand can cause the cue to drag during delivery.

36) Racking and Playing Various Versions of Billiards

Eight-ball (standard)

Start with any ball in the front, except the eight ball. Then work your way up one side of the triangle, alternating solid (commonly called "the little ones") with striped (commonly called "the big ones"). The eight ball goes in the middle. The two balls behind the eight can be either stripes or solids. What matters is that the outside perimeter alternates between little ones and big ones (they're actually the same size).

This is the racking pattern used in the vast majority of bars and rec rooms across the country, although official billiard rules require only the eight ball in the middle and alternating balls at the back corner. This won't be an issue unless you're shooting against a snob. In this case, you can use either the standard or official pattern—depends on who's holding the bigger stick at the time.

Roll the racked balls forward until the front ball is centered on the rack mark. If you place the rack too far forward, even an inch, the breaking pattern will be disrupted, resulting in fewer balls made on break. Most experienced pool players know this, and they won't like it.

Roll the rack back and forth a few times, position the lead ball directly over the mark, and then center the rack so the back edge is parallel with the back rail. Now, holding the rack in place with your thumbs and pinkies, slide your index and middle fingers from both hands behind the back row

A tight, properly set rack of balls makes for a more enjoyable game.

of balls. This packs the balls together, resulting in what's called a tight rack. This increases breaking power, which makes for a cleaner, faster game.

When the balls are set, carefully slide the rack up. Sometimes the lead ball will roll forward slightly when you remove the rack. If this happens, just rerack the balls, center and position the rack again, and then tap the lead ball with the cue ball or a ball from the back of the rack. This will stop that maddening forward roll.

Nine-ball

Nine-ball uses a diamond-shaped rack. The nine ball is in the middle, and the one ball is in the front of the diamond. Alternate big and little ones as you would for an eight-ball rack.

Nine-ball is played as a numerically sequential game. Simply, that means that you must make the balls in order, from lowest to highest. One ball first, then the two, and so on. This is why the one ball has to be in front of the rack—it has to be the first ball the breaker hits. Some versions allow using combinations, such as a one ball into a nine ball for an instant win, others don't. Just ask your opponent if you're not sure.

If you want to play nine-ball and don't have a nine-ball rack, you can use a triangular eight-ball rack and simply press the back half of the diamond into place with your hands. It's a fun game.

Cutthroat

Cutthroat pool is great if you have an uneven number of players, such as three or five, though you can play it with any number. You split teams up, then draw for your ball numbers. Keep your numbers secret. If you're playing with three people, one person would get balls one through five, another six through ten, and the last eleven through fifteen. You'll want to sink everybody else's balls and leave yours on the table—that's all there is to it. If you have an even number of people, the undrawn balls are dummies that anyone can hit in. Rack it the same as you would for eight-ball, except the eight ball doesn't have to be in the middle.

 Breaking

The setting couldn't have been more rustic; an outback country bar filled with mounted fish, old beer signs, and a curious collection of heavily paunched, bearded onlookers. It was our first night of pool league, my first game with my new team, and a flip of the quarter had decreed I would start it all off.

The fellow racking the balls took his time, and I marveled at how quiet everybody was. It didn't seem all that interesting, but I guess neither was the PBS documentary on the fuzzy screen behind the bar.

Finally my opponent stepped back, the brightly colored balls resting in a perfect triangle. I chalked the pool cue until my shoes were covered with blue dust, and then stepped up to the table, took aim (not careful aim, mind you) and struck a mighty blow that barely nicked the edge of the cue ball. The cue ball skittered weakly down one side, bounced off the side rail, and came to rest against the racked balls.

Some of them, I'm proud to say, separated by as much as a quarter-inch before rocking back into an almost-perfect triangle again.

Quite a start.

Billiards is a pretty common bar game, but it can take years to master. Most people don't spend all that much time practicing, yet when we do play it's usually in front of a group of people, some who take it quite seriously. Like many other things in guys' social clubs, that first impression is one of the most important.

A weak break looks, well, weak. Yet most kids can break a rack of balls nicely, which goes to show it's not really a matter of strength. Power is nice, yes, but it's by no means a necessity—we've all seen the skinny guy who jacks home runs and the uncoordinated giant who dribbles grounders to second base. My petite sisters, whom I outweigh by about a hundred pounds, often make better breaks than I do (a good break, for our purposes, means basically sending the balls flying in all directions, resulting in an open table). Weak breaks leave the balls clumped together, which makes for poor shooting opportunities and a slow, frustrating game.

Breaking is all about a smooth stroke and making a solid connection with the cue ball. Place the cue ball somewhere behind the second diamond marker, on the end of the table farthest from the rack. Many people offset the cue ball to one side, usually toward their dominant hand.

You can usually get the smoothest stroke by using your index and middle fingers on your nondominant hand to guide the free end of the cue. Wrapping your index finger around the end of the cue works well for subsequent shots, but during breaking it acts as a drag on the end of the cue, resulting in glancing blows or outright misses.

Now, draw an imaginary line from the center of the lead ball to the cue ball. Align the pool cue with that line, extending it back behind you. Make several false passes along that line, focusing on hitting the cue ball exactly in the center. When you're ready, simply concentrate on hitting that spot on the cue ball—forget about the balls behind it. Just hit it smoothly, and good things will happen.

A few more etiquette points on breaking:

1. Don't walk in front of someone who is about to break (at the other end of the table). This is akin to walking in front of someone while he's putting. Keep your voice down, or better yet, just shut the hell up for a second.

2. If you're playing repetitive matches with an opponent, the loser racks and winner usually breaks. If you've put up your quarters to play the winner of an ongoing match, you rack and your opponent breaks.

3. Sometimes making the eight ball on the break shot counts as an automatic win. Some people count it as an automatic loss. I've seen fights start over this—if money's on the line, establish this before you start.

 38 Calling Your Shot—When and How

Few experienced billiard players play slop pool (anything goes, as long as one of your balls goes in), yet most of them don't bother calling their shot. Why? Well, it's pretty obvious what you're attempting to do. In fact, all you usually have to do is call out your more difficult shots, such as banks and combinations. Calling your shot isn't a big deal with the vast majority of people you'll play against, since the honor system is still relied on around most pool tables.

In some tournaments, all you have to do is call your pocket. It doesn't matter how the ball gets there, as long as you hit one of your balls first, and the number you call drops in the right pocket. Bar or league rules can be a bit more vigorous. For example, if you're planning on hitting the three ball into a corner pocket, but think it'll touch the fifteen ball first, then you would say, "Three in the corner, off the fifteen." Now, if you hit the three ball into the corner pocket, *but miss the fifteen ball entirely*, you lose your turn. You have to hit *everything* you call, even if you make the ball you were trying to hit. Conversely, not calling the deflection and hitting it means you lose your turn, too.

Many people won't verbally call their shots at all. Faced with a difficult shot, they'll simply tap the pocket they're going for with the end of the pool cue. It's considered pretty bad form to ask them aloud to clarify their shot. Again, it's the honor system.

The following is some of the lingo people use when calling shots and determining penalties.

- **Walk(ing) the Dog:** A shot that's made by hitting the side of the ball with the cue ball, resulting in the ball rolling a long distance parallel to a rail.
- **Double Kiss:** The cue ball will hit a game ball twice, in quick succession.
- **Off the . . . :** This means the ball in question will touch another ball before dropping in the pocket; for example, the twelve ball off the nine in the side. The twelve ball will glance off the nine and then go into the side pocket.
- **Scratch:** The cue ball goes into the pocket after you shoot at a ball. In bar rules, the opposing player can place the cue ball anywhere behind an invisible line between the second diamonds (at the opposite end of the table where the balls were racked). In tournaments, your opponent can put the ball anywhere. A scratch can also mean hitting the eight ball in before all your balls are gone (an automatic loss).

 39 Putting English on the Cue Ball

I vividly remember watching my dad playing pool in the little country tavern when I was a kid. He was a fine shot in the traditional sense, but what I remember the most was how he could curve the cue ball around one ball to hit another behind it, almost as though the cue ball were on a string. It's the kind of stuff you usually only see with trick shots on ESPN2 nowadays, but the use of English, or controlled spin, is an essential part of any pool player's arsenal.

English is primarily used to position your cue ball for a follow-up shot, or to avoid scratches. By striking the cue ball at different positions you can make it stop, roll forward, go to either side, or even reverse directions. Done correctly, this means you can position the cue ball in a spot that gives you an excellent chance at sinking another ball. Most good pool players plan at least two or three shots in advance; professionals can look at a table after the break and see all eight shots they need for a win.

The first step toward using English is conditioning the cue tip. Scuff it thoroughly and chalk the bejesus out of it. Applying English with a smooth, hard tip is nearly impossible.

The most common way to use English is to make the cue ball stop dead when it makes contact with the game ball. This is very useful when the game ball is near the pocket and you have a straight-on shot, since hitting the cue ball with a normal stroke will cause you to scratch. To stop the cue ball on contact, simply hit it crisply about two-thirds of the way down.

To get backspin, hit it the same way described above, but angle the back of the stick slightly up and punch the tip through the ball – don't stop the stick once you make the initial contact. This works best on close shots, since backspin usually slows or disappears completely after the cue ball travels a couple of feet across the felt.

For forward English, hit the cue ball high, about a third of the way down, and follow through with an exaggerated motion. This is an under-utilized technique for getting the cue ball out of a crammed area, or even breaking up a clump of balls after your shot. For right English, hit the ball on the right side, and vice versa for left English. A cue ball with side English will rarely move at right angles, but instead will move diagonally upon hitting the game ball. Again, punch the cue tip through the ball with an exaggerated follow-through.

English is also useful for hitting the cue ball off the rail for bank shots. By putting side English on the cue ball, you can get it to change angles when it touches the rail.

 ## Arm-wrestling a Stronger Opponent

I knew they were trouble as soon as they walked into the bar.

It was Taco Tuesday—all you could eat tacos and all you could drink margaritas for ten bucks. Looking back, I'm pretty sure that night was sponsored by Pepto-Bismol. AJ had just finished racking the pool table when one of the guys asked if we were interested in playing doubles. Maybe, you know, put a little wager on it?

"Sure," AJ said. "We're playing like crap, though."

"Perfect," he said, smiling at us with all three teeth.

We really were playing like crap, probably because of the oversized margaritas. The people we were up against, big tattooed men with hard faces, looked like they were probably born with a pool cue clenched in one hairy fist. We figured we'd play one set and rotate out of the game.

I'm not sure how many times we missed the first few games. Not too many, that's for damn sure. A window had opened for us, as it will open over the course of the night for certain people, and our particular window seemed about the size of a barn door. Bank shots, combos, you name it; everything we tried we made.

Our opponents weren't amused.

"Playing like crap, huh?" one of them asked AJ after our third or fourth win. He was six-two, at least two-fifty, with military tats plastered down his thick forearms. His friends called him Chief. "I'm out of money."

"That's all right," AJ said carelessly. "We can play this next one just for pride."

It's a strange thing when a bar goes silent all at once. You'd swear that everyone is engrossed in their own conversations, that the jukebox would drown out a few insignificant words. Not so. In the space of a few seconds, the only sounds were the distant wailing of Hank Jr. and the slow gurgle of the taco meat in its crock-pot.

"Pride?" Chief asked heavily.

"Well, you know, maybe that's the wrong word," AJ conceded. "For fun, how about?"

He stared hard at AJ, then pulled on the chain attached to his wallet. He opened up his billfold and extracted a greasy-looking dollar bill. "That's what I got left. I'll play you for that dollar on this pool table, but it ain't going to be with a stick in my hand. I'll arm-wrestle you for it."

AJ didn't miss a beat. "Oh, I don't arm-wrestle," he said, then turned and pointed at me. "But he does."

Chief squinted down the length of the table. "That right?"

"Sure," I said. What can I say—tequila makes you do strange things.

"Right here," he said, pointing at the table.

I walked over, added my dollar to the table, and locked grips.

I knew immediately that Chief was stronger than me. It didn't matter. In under a minute I was a buck richer and our surly pool opponents—about a half-dozen in all—had exited the bar.

You don't have to be stronger than your opponent to beat him at arm wrestling. You can't be a *lot* weaker, of course—let's not descend into *Revenge of the Nerds* territory. You'll need to be within about 25 percent of your opponent's upper body strength to have a shot at winning, though not necessarily their arm strength. A lot of arm-wrestling power is rooted in hand, wrist, and shoulder musculature. The results are also heavily dependent on technique, and the technique you'll use depends on the relative strength of you and your opponent.

There are a couple of ways to figure out strength beforehand. Shake hands to get a feel for your opponent's hand strength, and take a quick look at his forearms and biceps to get an indication of general arm strength. Don't worry overmuch about his upper arm. While it certainly makes things tougher, an opponent with big biceps isn't the kiss of death.

Now you'll need to come to grips with your opponent at the table. This is no time for a weak grip; many arm-wrestling matches get bogged down in virtual stalemates, so having a psychological edge is important. This means acting like you're just getting warmed up at any point during the match, even if you've just popped a couple of veins and are trying desperately not to cry. It also means squeezing hell out of your opponent's hand.

Circle your nonwrestling thumb and index finger around your opponent's elbow. He should do the same (assuming you aren't at an arm-wrestling table). This locks your elbows in place, preventing them from sliding. Don't let your opponent lift up your elbow, since this will result in a tremendous loss of power on your side; you're basically a lever without a fulcrum as soon as your elbow leaves the table.

You'll usually have a referee, who will place his hands over your combined grip. When he lets go the match begins, and the match is almost always won in the first five to ten seconds. Even if it actually goes on for a quarter-hour, both people are pretty sure how things are going to turn out within those first crucial moments. Hit your opponent with everything you have as soon as you can, since it's much harder to work uphill once you get down.

There are three basic techniques, depending on whether you feel you're stronger or weaker than your opponent.

The Hook

This is the standard arm-wrestling strategy used by most non-diehards. The technique is simple, but there are some subtle intricacies that can greatly improve your record. Use a hook with an opponent you feel is the same strength, or weaker, than you.

The very first thing you need to establish is hand-angle dominance. In simpler words, force your opponent's hand back and expose his wrist. Once his wrist is back, he's forced to use a

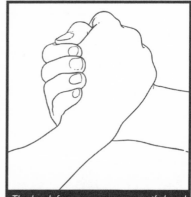

The hook forces your opponent's hand back, increasing your power and leverage.

different set of muscles to push against your arm pressure. To understand this better, grab your forearm just below the elbow, then make a fist and bend your wrist back and forth. You can feel the muscles shift according to your wrist position. Your stronger muscles are in the bottom part of your forearm, which is why using the hook technique is so important.

Try to pull your opponent's hand toward you. This is called backpressure, and it helps tremendously, maybe more than any other single technique. A straight arm exerts more pressure, which is why arm-wrestling short-armed people sucks; they inherently have a more vertical stance. But you can pull them toward you to counter their natural advantage, which will stretch their arm out and weaken their leverage.

Toproll

The toproll is a fairly advanced technique that allows you to beat stronger opponents. It's best to practice the grip movement and application of backpressure beforehand, so it doesn't seem like a rehearsed move. Besides, you'll need to quickly perform the toproll before your stronger opponent slams your arm down.

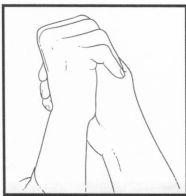

The toproll is a great technique when facing an obviously stronger opponent.

The key is to work your hand up your opponent's grip by walking your fingers up through your opponent's palm. Done successfully, your hand will wrap around the top part of his hand and he'll be stuck holding your wrist or the bottom part of your hand. Apply as much backpressure as possible, and you can beat pretty much anybody in the bar (in your approximate strength range). Both the hook and the toproll benefit greatly from a third technique, which is actually more of a finishing move, called the press.

The Press

This is the technique I used to beat Chief. Basically, it involves rotating your body so that your shoulder and body weight are in line with the direction you want your arm to go.

Unless your opponent is extremely strong, he'll be unable to move your whole body unless he rotates against you. Easy enough, but many people take the term *arm-wrestling* literally, and won't use their body, even when they see you doing it.

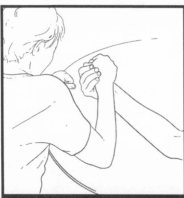

The press technique: By pivoting your body, you can use the force of your entire upper body to whup a stronger opponent.

It's perfectly acceptable to use this technique, and also a perfect way to finish off a stubborn opponent.

41 Losing an Arm-wrestling Match Gracefully

If you arm-wrestle frequently anywhere besides the local junior high school, there'll be plenty of times when you find yourself pinned three-quarters of the way down, with no way up. Once you realize you can't win, it's time to call the game and go get a beer.

Don't let your arm go limp. Your opponent may very well slam your hand down and walk away, and that ain't cool (for you, anyways). Most of the time all you have to do is look your opponent in the eye and nod once. Usually he'll straighten up, and you can let him push you down the rest of the way. Many times you'll disengage and then come back together for a quick handshake. There's no need to be surly; even the best arm wrestlers in the world lose several matches every year.

Even if you're on the winning side, feel free to offer up a compliment. Calling your opponent tough isn't a bad idea, and it pays to remember that you may not necessarily be stronger than the person you just whipped—especially if you relied heavily on technique. But he doesn't know you're not as tough as you seemed, so it doesn't hurt to be gracious. It might even save you another wrestling match later on in the night.

42 Fisticuffs—Giving

I'm not a fighter. This doesn't mean I've never been in a fight, of course. It means that I'm a decent-sized guy who gets mellow instead of ornery when I drink, I don't flirt with other guys' women, and I rarely talk trash (I like to talk smart, though). Besides, I think people who *like* to fight are morons. There is very little satisfaction in hurting another person, even a dyed-in-the-wool asshole. And if you're a fairly strong person, there's always the possibility of causing permanent damage, death, or lawsuits. Plus, it fouls your hand up something awful when you hit someone in the head.

And then there's the flip side. There are bad people out there, people who will hurt you in any way, shape, or form available to them. To assume these people will fight fairly, or refrain from using a cue stick or beer bottle, is a surefire way to end up in the hospital or morgue. Unfortunately, walking away from a fight is difficult for guys, who often feel passivity constitutes weakness. Yet the best advice is also the simplest: Don't fight unless you absolutely have to.

Sometimes, though, it comes down to fists, and there's just no getting around it. And while the best advice is avoidance, the second-best advice is to be totally pissed off. Going into a fight half-assed is a surefire way to get your front teeth handed to you. There is no gray area; fight hard or not at all.

Watch just about any action movie, and you'll see the hero use all sorts of uppercuts, roundhouses, and big looping punches to knock out his enemies. The only punch you, Joe Streetfighter, need is a jab. Sounds weak, but you have to remember you're not wearing boxing gloves. A simple jab, thrown straight from the shoulder, hurts like hell when it lands. And just like a straight thrust in fencing, it's the hardest punch to block. Nearly every amateur fight I've ever been involved in or witnessed has involved more wrestling than boxing, and a jab is also the easiest punch to administer in close quarters fighting. A compact uppercut is also effective, though generally difficult to bring past your opponent's chest. Many fights end up on the ground, and it's tough to bring those big roundhouses into effect when you're rolling around in the parking lot.

It's a rare person who can end a fight with a single punch. A jab can be quickly repeated, and multiple throws are pretty much the name of the game. Two or three well-placed jabs can calm down even the most unruly drunk or loudmouthed, aggressive punk. If you need proof of how effective jabs are, watch a hockey game. These guys know how to bare-knuckle fight, and you'll rarely see a big looping swing. They keep their elbows tucked in and their swings compact, economical. They're also pretty damn effective at drawing blood in a short time frame.

Make sure you don't tuck your thumb into your palm when you make a fist. If you hit someone like this, the only thing you're going to break is your thumb. Worse, you won't want to hit the person you're fighting again—but he may not be ready to quit. And for God's sake, keep your wrist straight. Bending your wrist up when you punch looks silly and doesn't work, yet lots of inexperienced fighters do this very thing, usually out of panic.

A lot of people equate that angled wrist with a sissy punch, but the real difference between a punch and a sissy punch is the action of your shoulders and hips. A sissy punch is arm-only. A real punch is simply an extension of your body mass, flung through your hips and shoulders and extended into your arm. By harnessing all the weight of your body, even a 120-pound kid can land a serious blow.

Listen, you should only throw a punch as a last resort. But when you feel like you're in danger, when there's no way out of trading blows, hit first and hit hard. It takes a helluva lot to stop certain people, and you never know whom you're up against. People get killed and seriously hurt in fights all the time, so this isn't a recommendation to beat someone senseless. The legal and moral arguments against that are obvious and I won't even attempt to address them here. But if someone's going to get hurt, it shouldn't be you. Hit them hard enough to take away their desire to grapple with you, and both of you can wake up in the morning with only minor regrets.

Bottom line: Fight only if you have to, but if you have to, don't be a victim. Hit hard, hit fast, and then get the hell out of there.

And don't punch like a girl.

(43) Fisticuffs—Receiving

You better know what time it is before you get in a fight. No, don't look at your watch—look at the guy you're about to fight. If he's not wearing a watch, see which hand he's using to hold his drink. The cleanest punches I've seen have come from lefties (who, incidentally, wear their watch on their right wrist and usually hold their drink in their left hand). Most people don't understand that the southpaw they've just insulted is already in a fighting stance. They're still waiting for the person to rotate when suddenly the punch comes flying out of nowhere and they end up with a bloody lip.

Regardless of your opponent's dominant arm, it's essential that you don't wait for a punch to come to you. Your odds are much better if you're aggressive, or at least moving instead of just standing there. If possible, immediately circle toward your opponent's dominant hand. This shortens and weakens any punch he can throw at you. Protect your groin, gut, and eyes—getting hit in any of these places can end a fight and mark the beginning of a beating. If you do get hit in the gut or groin, swivel away instead of bending down, which is a great way to end up with a knee to the face.

Usually the best defense is a good offense. Throwing punches at your opponent's face will keep him disoriented and affect his aim and depth judgment. This is why most street fights end up with about a 5 percent hit rate; each guy is so busy avoiding the other guy's punches that he rushes his own punches. This is generally a good thing for both parties. After all, there's a simple reason bare-knuckle fighting was banned.

These tips might help, but sooner or later you're going to get hit. It hurts. It hurts *badly*.

Get over it.

This isn't just tough guy talk. It's easy to get paralyzed when someone lands a hard punch, and there will be a desire to retreat, to duck and cover until you can recover. This is the worst way to recover, actually. You need to forget about the pain, to turn it into anger that you can use to your advantage. Shake it off. Hell, give him a bloody smile and wade back in. Sometimes this is more unnerving than landing a telling punch of your own. Don't freak out—people have been hitting each other ever since Gorg took more than his share of mammoth meat.

Move with your opponent's punch. This seems obvious and is usually an instinctive avoidance responsive. Nevertheless, many people move into a punch, that is, they lead with their chin, and these are the people who get knocked down with single punches. If you need to move into the other fighter's space, cover your face and tense your stomach muscles. But unless you're a martial arts guru, moving straight toward your opponent is risky. It's like shooting decoy ducks—all your opponent has to do is lean back and fire away.

If you hit the ground, roll out of the way and get up immediately. Don't expect mercy—expect to get hit or kicked while you're down. If you are getting smacked around, now might be the time to quit boxing and start wrestling. In other words, tackle your opponent, which will reduce the effectiveness of his punches. Go for his waist, not his legs; it's too easy for someone to shake a leg free and put the boots to you. Taking a fight to the ground also softens the blows you'll receive, which is sort of an added bonus. Of course, the trick here is to avoid being pinned, where your opponent can punch you in various places at his leisure.

Bottom line: If you throw a punch, one or more is going to be thrown back at you. If you're scared or angry enough, most punches you take will be manageable. Not pleasant, but manageable. If you're looking to liven up a dull night by being a jerk and picking a fight, those punches are going to hurt a lot more. And that's a lesson all in itself.

SECTION 3

Outdoors

Building a Fire in Shitty Weather

A lot of guys pride themselves on being able to build a campfire. They gather up their newspaper and cardboard, their kindling and their dry, split wood, and head down to the campfire ring with their butane lighter. A few minutes later it's s'mores time, and everybody's happy. This isn't a bad thing. I've done it myself, on more than one occasion.

But these are leisure fires. When you really need a fire, when you're wet or cold, a fire isn't just something to melt marshmallows and chocolate over. It's a source of life, a means of preventing hypothermia and frostbite. This is almost always the time when a fire is the most difficult to build. There may be snow on the ground, or it might be raining with a strong wind. At times like these, it's essential to know where and how to build a fire quickly.

The first and perhaps most important decision is where to locate your fire. In some cases this will be an easy decision, or circumstances will demand that you build a fire at a certain spot. But if you have a choice, build the fire behind some type of windbreak, such as a large boulder or a deadfall. Locate your fire four to six feet away from the windbreak; the area between the fire and the windbreak will be the warmest spot once everything gets going, and you'll want to be able to occupy it.

Forget the panoramic view and locate the fire close to a decent supply of firewood. If you don't have an axe or handsaw, this means an area of the forest where there's plenty of deadfalls. Many times the densest stands of forest have the highest supply of dead wood, since overcrowding tends to kill off some of the trees. If you've read Jack London, you know to not build a fire under a snow-laden pine tree. The fire can heat up the snow, sending it cascading down to smother your fire. In fact, never build a fire under any pine tree, as they can go up in flames in seconds.

Now that you have a location picked out, try to find some hand-sized rocks for the fire bed (not the traditional fire ring). A properly constructed fire bed facilitates airflow under your fire, much like grating in a wood furnace. This also elevates your fire, reducing contact with damp ground or snow. If you can't locate any rocks, situate some sticks in a row for your fire's base, leaving small gaps between the wood.

Now you need to find some kindling. If it's wet out, much of the ground material is going to be impossible to light. Two easy sources of

Rocks forming bed, not ring

Snow

Gaps in fire bed for airflow

Instead of a traditional fire ring, lay a bed of stones down as a bed to elevate your fire and increase air flow during those critical early stages of the fire.

elevated kindling are birch bark and the small dead branches found at the base of mature pines. These two materials are common in much of North America and will light in even the wettest conditions. Birch bark is naturally resistant to water (think birch-bark canoes) and is extremely flammable. The branches at the base of mature pines remain relatively sheltered for years, since the pine tree acts as a huge umbrella. These dead sticks make for excellent kindling. Rotted stumps or logs can also be kicked apart to reveal the dry and often crumbly interiors. These chunks of wood, sometimes scored with insect tunnels, also make excellent kindling in any weather.

Gather enough wood to last at least an hour before you light the kindling, since fledgling fires often fizzle out if left untended during that crucial first stage. The smallest, most flammable kindling goes on the bed of rocks or sticks, with small twigs leaning against each other in a pyramid. The pyramid technique allows the finder—be it newspaper, cardboard, or bark—to remain loose and uncompressed. Again, this increases airflow, allowing the fire to catch and expand quickly.

Light the fire from the bottom at several locations, to produce a short, intense burst of flame. Waterproof matches or a butane lighter wrapped in a sealed plastic baggie have saved many lives over the years, and it's always a good idea to carry one or the other when you're venturing into the woods.

Larger kindling goes over the base kindling, again in a pyramid style. Don't put any heavy stuff on until the smaller material catches, and then only carefully. You don't want to crush the air flow. Be patient, and make sure you have enough smaller kindling to catch that initial wave of fire. A successful fire is built in incremental steps, moving slowly up through kindling sizes until you have arm-sized wood burning steadily.

In extremely cold weather, build an additional two or three fires in a circle, and then sit in the center. This method will warm you up much quicker than huddling over a single, larger blaze. If you're forced to spend the night and the ground is cold or frozen, build a secondary fire over the area where you plan to sleep. When you get sleepy, put the fire out and sleep on top of the fire-warmed earth. If you don't have the resources to build another fire, use pine boughs or dead grass as a rough mattress to get off the cold, heat-robbing ground.

 **45 Tracking**

It was a cold winter day, and I had my quarry nestled squarely in the sights of my twelve-gauge shotgun. I fired and saw a puff of hide fly as the slug hit home, exactly where I had aimed. The animal dropped to its knees, and I breathed a sigh of relief. The sigh hadn't even left my lips when the animal jumped up and ran off, leaving me standing there in slack-jawed surprise. By the time I recovered enough to think about taking a second shot, I realized my shotgun was jammed.

AJ ran up to me and followed my gaze out over the snow-covered field. "What the hell happened?"

"Damned if I know," I said, watching as the animal stopped and glared at us from a quarter-mile away. "I hit it right where I aimed. I think the slug bounced off." We watched as the big animal turned and trotted into a swamp, a thick tangle of spruce floating over a bed of deep moss, and looked at each other like kids who have just started up a piece of machinery they can't turn off.

After a brief consult with my dad, we retired the slug gun and broke out the long-range deer rifles. There was fresh snow on the ground, so it was easy to find the animal's path. We split up on each side of the track once we hit the swamp, trying to keep the spooked critter between us. We quickly lost sight of each other in the thick trees and brush, and we weren't paying much attention to the tracks, either. After all, it had to be somewhere close.

"Go on out the end!" I shouted to AJ when we were halfway through the swamp. "I'll push it to you!"

"Okay!" he shouted back.

I cut to my left to pick up the track. In the deep bed of moss, the tracks were just giant holes, impossible to identify, but headed right toward AJ. "He's coming!" I shouted, expecting to hear AJ's shot any moment. But when the trees thinned and I saw AJ standing there, right in line with the tracks I was following, I couldn't believe it had slipped past us. I actually looked up in a tree.

"Where'd it go?" I asked.

AJ shook his head. "Not by me." I glanced down at the tracks I was following again and groaned. The moss had thinned out at the edge of the swamp, revealing more detail in the tracks. What I thought were animal tracks were actually size-eleven boot tracks.

I had been tracking my brother-in-law.

A few minutes later we picked up the right set of tracks and followed them for about a half-mile. Sensing we were getting close, we split up again, but this time we kept each other in sight. We went about another fifty yards, then walked around a little bunch of thick spruce. We were just past it when we heard something crash through the undergrowth behind us and disappear into a patch of alders.

"That's one smart animal," AJ said.

I nodded agreement. AJ circled around, trying to push it back to me. He reappeared twenty cold minutes later, shaking his head. "It's somewhere inside that circle I just made."

"Sure it didn't slip past you?"

"No chance."

AJ took off on pressing business, but promised to return in fifteen minutes. Too cold and impatient to sit there and wait, I slowly walked through the brush and picked up the trail, the large tracks headed due east. I moved slowly, searching for the next track before I took a step. About a hundred yards in I saw an exceptionally clear hoof print, less than two inches away from an exceptionally clear size-eleven boot mark. No chance it slipped by you, eh AJ?

AJ reappeared a few minutes later, startling the animal into a headlong rush back toward me. It stopped once to look back, and like Lot's wife, the results were just as disastrous. When we walked over to our prize, AJ lifted its head out of the snow by its horns and let out a victory whoop.

Yup, quite a way to butcher our first steer.

Yeah, it was a steer. A smart steer, but a steer nonetheless. Both AJ and I are fairly experienced outdoorsmen, and neither of us are exceptionally stupid. Both of us have tracked deer, coyotes, and other critters for long distances. So how did this happen? How did we repeatedly lose the trail of a 1,000-pound domestic animal in fresh snow?

Well, we rushed into it. When we took over butchering duties for my father, things didn't go as planned. We tried to fix our mistake, and we tried to fix it fast. This meant rushing over the trail, which essentially means breaking most of the rules for successful tracking. You can't rush a trail unless you have absolutely perfect conditions, and then only at your own peril. It's easy to assume you can't lose the track, only to have it disappear, or end up tracking the wrong animal (or your brother-in-law). Since there is often adrenaline flowing during a tracking situation, it's easy to rush things.

You have to slow down. The trail as you first approach it is unbroken, as clear as it will ever be. Don't ruin that by stamping back and forth. Always mark the location you first saw the animal by noting two or three landmarks, a process commonly referred to as triangulation. This is an extremely useful tool to locate an area first viewed from a distance. Once you locate the first track, look for the second, third, and so on. This will establish a line of travel, which can be deceiving from a distance. Then mark the location of the first track. Just shove a stick into the ground, or hang a glove from a tree. That way you'll always have a starting point if you lose the track. Keep doing this each time the terrain changes into less trackable conditions—such as a stretch of dry ground or the confluence of other tracks.

Walk parallel to the tracks, close enough to see them clearly but not on top of them. If you lose sight of the tracks, mark the last track and then move out in increasing circles until you pick it up again. Don't rush. In fact, if you're applying this tracking technique to a hunting situation, you shouldn't even begin tracking until thirty minutes after your shot, since an animal that's pushed after a shot will go much farther than an animal allowed to rest and stiffen up.

Most wounded animals will head downhill and/or into thick cover. If there's a sizable creek or river nearby, most animals will instinctively head toward it, even if they're a mile or more away. In some cases, it's a good idea to circle ahead of the animal if it looks like it's going to cross a river that you can't. Otherwise, move slowly and don't leave the trail.

If you end up tracking in the dark, a lantern is much more effective than a flashlight. The soft, even light works well to pick up blood spoor, and it casts a wider sphere of light than a narrow-beamed flashlight.

If you're tracking without snow and without blood spoor, things get tough in a hurry. Following broken blades of grass or overturned pebbles is the stuff of fiction for most amateur trackers. Instead, try to determine a line of movement for the animal, then concentrate on those areas where it's possible to pick up a track (e.g., a muddy flat or a meadow of tall grass that will bend as the animal passes). Look for overturned leaves, which are often easy to spot in older-growth forests, since they expose bare earth when the animal passes by. This sporadic tracking technique can be tricky, but it often works if you have a basic understanding of what's driving the animal. Is it fear? Hunger? Anxiety? Maybe the need to mate? Stop and think about the reasons the animal is moving and where it might find what it's after. Then use the trackable areas to confirm or reject your hypothesis.

Remember also that tracking conditions can dictate how long you have to track. Falling snow means great tracking, but if you fall too far behind, the tracks will fill in. The same principle applies to heavy frost or dew, which will disappear as the day wears on. Adjust your tracking rate accordingly.

 46 Pitching a Tent

We were freshly arrived in the Colorado mountains after an eighteen-hour drive, and we were tired, eye-weary, and needed a nap worse than we needed a shower, and we needed a shower pretty damn bad.

I had a brand new wall tent, bought especially for this trip, and as soon as we rolled to a stop at the primitive campground, we started putting it together. After 1,000 miles of blurry road signs and high beams, putting pole AB into slot 32 while maintaining contact with flap B12 wasn't pretty. Our first few efforts looked like a tent Picasso might paint while deep in his cups, but we finally put it together in a roughly pentagonal shape. I think it made it a couple of hours before it collapsed on top of us, convincing my sleep-deprived friend a grizzly bear was attacking us.

To avoid campsite frustration, put your tent together in your yard first. Purchase a pack of different-colored tapes or paints beforehand, then give each joint a unique color. Later, when the time comes to pitch your tent after a long hike, your tired mind can just follow the color scheme instead of the directions, which tend to be written in small print by an illiterate guy who flunked out of engineering school.

Most tents come with a two-tier roof system. The peak will be vented, and the rain fly will suspend slightly over the screened vent. This keeps rain out, while still allowing condensation to exit the tent, so be sure to adjust the rain fly correctly. Otherwise you might have an inadvertent shower (no rain fly) or sauna (rain fly not suspended high enough) in your tent.

Set up your tent on high, level ground. It is an immutable law of nature that rain will fall within four hours of tent pitching, and any small depression will accumulate water. This means a midnight soaking. If you're really unlucky, high winds will accompany that downpour, which can flatten an unsecured tent in seconds. String guy wires to stakes or tree bases from each corner. Believe me, you don't want to wake up at three in the morning with a face full of wet nylon. Well, sometimes this isn't such a bad thing, but . . . never mind.

Make sure you clear the tent base of rocks and branches. This not only prevents the bottom of the tent from ripping, but also makes for a more comfortable night's sleep. If it's cold out and you don't have a cot or air mattress, pile dead grass or pine boughs underneath the tent; you'll stay much warmer if you avoid direct contact with the ground.

Finally, be sure to locate your campfire upwind and at least ten to fifteen feet away from your tent. This prevents smoke from saturating your tent, and eliminates the possibility of a tent fire; sparks can quickly ignite even "fireproof" tent material, with disastrous results. The safest bet is to extinguish your fire when you go to bed, but many people like to watch their campfire as they nod off. Just keep the fire a safe distance away from the tent and don't add a bunch of fuel before you go to sleep.

 Cleaning a Fish

There's an old saying along the lines of "if you catch it, you clean it." Fair enough, but it often seems easier catching that elusive fish than producing a boneless fillet. Actually, cleaning a fish is easy and sort of fun. It just takes a little practice. And while there are several different ways to clean a fish, from a simple gill-and-gut to the boneless fillet, none of them are very difficult.

Gutting and gilling is a part of steaking, so we'll cover that technique first. Even if you plan on filleting the fish later, gilling and gutting helps preserve flavor and prevent spoilage. Cut from the vent upward until you reach the jaw, being careful to cut only deep enough to sever the muscle tissue and not the guts. Then pull everything out. What, you thought you weren't going to get your hands dirty? Is you a man, or is you a hand model? Rip 'em out of there. The kidneys are two long strips of bloodlike material near the top of the abdominal cavity, along each side of the spine. Use your knife to scrape them off, then reach in and pull the gills out, or just cut the whole head off. Once the guts and head/gills are gone, simply cut the fish crossways to steak it out.

If you're going to grill or smoke the fish, this is all you have to do. Unfortunately, this technique is not the most eater-friendly version of fish cleaning. However, it works great to preserve every ounce of flavorful meat on smaller fish like sunfish or stream trout, which are notoriously hard to fillet without wasting meat. To remove sunfish scales, use a fish scaler or spoon to scrape off the scales, working from the tail toward the head. Then fry or grill the fish with the skin attached. The skin is edible and actually pretty tasty. This won't work with catfish, trout, or any other fish that lacks larger scales.

That leaves us with the boneless fillet. Nothing but mouthfuls of sweet, crumbly goodness. This is the best way to eat fish, and also the most involved cleaning technique. Not hard, mind you, just more involved than other methods.

Lay the fish flat on its side. The knife goes in just behind the pectoral fin and the operculum, angled straight down or slightly toward the head. Cut into the fish until you reach the spine, then turn the blade so it's parallel with the backbone. Keeping the blade flat, run the knife along the spine, being careful to avoid cutting through the backbone. You should feel the knife cutting through the ribs, which will dull most fillet knives pretty quickly. Be sure to resharpen your knife after every two or three fish.

Stop about an inch before the base of the tail, right before the meat runs out. Then flip the fillet over, so the skin is facing down. Now slide the knife edge between the skin and the meat, just above the tail, and

Make your first cut just behind the gill plate, straight down to the backbone. Then turn the knife blade and cut down the backbone, flip the fillet over, and remove the skin.

gently saw your way up through the fillet. Keep pressure on the skin with the flat of the knife blade. You may want to press your free hand down on the skin to keep it from tearing. A gentle back and forth sawing motion works best to remove the skin from the fillet. You should end up with a hunk of skin still attached to the fish, and one skinless fillet.

Now slide the knife behind the rib cage of the fillet and cut out the ribs, keeping the knife edge pressed against the back of the ribcage to prevent waste. Some fish will have center bones behind the ribcage that run back to the tail, and other fish may have additional bones embedded in the fillet. Run your thumb back and forth over the fillet to find any bones that you missed. You might also want to remove the strip of dark red meat along the lateral line (straight down the middle of the outside of the fillet). This meat often has a strong, unpleasant taste. It's fairly soft, so just scrape it off with the knife edge.

Field Dressing and Quartering Large Game

Anyone who pulls the trigger on an animal better know how to clean it, and clean it quickly. You owe the animal that much. Prompt field dressing is essential in preserving taste and preventing spoilage, especially in warmer weather, but some hunters worry too much about the shot, and not enough about the plate.

You're going to get your hands bloody. Once you accept that, everything is pretty straightforward. Despite all the weekend warriors who walk around with Bowie knives strapped to their waists, there's actually not much heavy cutting involved. All you need is a three- to four-inch knife with a good, thick blade. A meat saw is nice, too.

Lay the animal so the belly is facing up or to the side. You may want to cut a branch long enough to prop the animal's rear legs open, which will make for easier cutting. Cut from the vent to the bottom of the rib cage, exactly in the middle of the belly—but don't cut deep! Cutting too deep will puncture internal organs, including the intestines, stomach, and bladder. The contents of these organs are not something you want on your steaks. Cut all the way around the vent, and lop off any dangling reproductive structures.

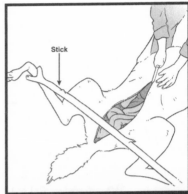

The first few cuts are the most critical. Work slowly, cutting through each layer carefully.

Cut through the meat above the pelvic arch to reveal the pelvic bone, which needs to be split or cut open. Since deer, elk, and moose have hard bones, you may need to use a small saw to cut through the pelvis. Sometimes it's possible to use the point of your knife as a wedge to split the pelvic bone, though this is tricky in older or heavy-boned animals.

Now that everything is opened up, all you have to do is pull the viscera—oh hell, let's just call them guts—out. Cut all the way around the vent in order to free the end of the large intestine. Everything below the diaphragm should pull free easily, though you may need to do a little cutting to free the kidneys and connective tissue. There should be more pulling than cutting. Use your knife to cut out the diaphragm, which is a large thin flap of muscle separating the guts from the heart and lungs, then cut the heart and lungs free (they're attached near the front of the chest cavity) and pull the whole works loose.

If you have a large animal on the ground, such as an elk or moose, and no vehicle nearby, you're going to need to quarter the animal before hauling it out. It's best to try and hang the animal from a tree before quartering (it's much easier to field dress them this way, too). A block and tackle set can be purchased for $20–$30 and is a great investment for any backcountry hunting outfit.

Remove the head just below the base of the skull, and then the legs at the knee joints. Starting from the tail, use a meat saw to cut through the exact middle of the spine, which will result in two equal halves. It's important to stay in the middle of the spine, even though it means lots of cutting. To quarter the animal, cut through the second or third rib from the bottom. If you have a really heavy animal, you can cut it into sixths or even eighths. If you're going to drag the quarters out, leave the hide on. Otherwise, skin the animal to reduce weight.

Once the animal is field dressed, move the meat to a cool location as soon as possible. Wild game is remarkably flavorful if handled and cooked correctly, but mistreatment at the initial stages of butchering can often result in a "gamy" taste. Just remember to dive in and get it cleaned—blood washes off.

 ## Chopping Down a Tree

Oh sure, any idiot with a Jonserud or Husqvarna can knock a tree down in a few seconds. The hard part is getting the tree to land where you want it to go.

Notching and felling a tree is a simple matter of sixth-grade physics, but every year people are killed when the tree they're cutting falls on top of them. Countless more wannabe lumberjacks drop trees on their cars, houses, neighbor's dog, and so forth. Great grist for funny home video shows, but pure hell on insurance premiums.

Assess the tree before you start cutting. Is it leaning in a direction you don't want it to go? Is it surrounded by other trees that might hang it up once it falls? Is it dead on top? If so, could the brittle upper section snap off once it starts to fall? The term for a tree like this is a *widow maker*, and they've killed a lot of would-be lumberjacks.

If possible, work with the unique conditions of each tree. If it's leaning hard to the south, drop it that way. If it grows straight up, but there's a strong wind (and don't underestimate wind power—the canopy of a tree can act like a sail, even if it's fairly calm at ground level), fell the tree in the same direction the wind is blowing. If you can't drop it the way conditions dictate—if, for example, there's a house in the way—attach two ropes as high up on the tree as possible, and have a couple of helpers pull on each rope at quartering angles. The tree should fall between them, but this can be tricky. Make sure your helpers are at least as far away as the tree is tall.

Cut a wedge out first, then cut down at an angle from the opposite side.

Okay, now that we know where we want the tree to go, let's knock this sucker down. First, make sure the area around the base of the tree is clear of underbrush, logs, or any other debris that might get in your way. No matter how well you plan, sometimes you just need to drop the chainsaw and run like hell. Cut the brush away and clear out any debris before you start working on the tree.

Never cut down a tree by sawing straight through, since the tree will lean forward and pinch the chainsaw bar between the stump and the still-standing tree. With a larger tree, it's almost impossible to free the bar of a stuck chainsaw without cutting the tree down with an axe or another chainsaw. Instead, notch out a wedge on the same side you want the tree to fall, no more than halfway through the tree. Remove the wedge, then simply cut down at an angle from the opposite side. The tree will usually fall in the direction of the wedge, although it's possible for it to fall in any direction. Stop often to push gently on the tree with your shoulder to guide it in the right direction when you're making the final cut. When it starts to fall, shut off the chainsaw and move away. Kickbacks, falling limbs, and an idling chainsaw are a recipe for disaster when trees start to fall.

Make sure the tree is all the way down before moving in for limbing and sectioning. Sometimes other trees, undergrowth, or the branches will keep the tree suspended for a moment before it actually comes to its final rest. These secondary falls are rarely fatal, but can crush a foot in an instant.

General Shooting Safety

If you never point a gun at another person, you will never accidentally kill a husband, a wife, a sister or brother, or a son or daughter. Simple enough. Never, ever raise the muzzle of your gun unless you are prepared for the gun to go off. Firearms aren't evil, and they aren't the salvation of Western civilization. They're just tools, and like any tool they'll cause serious damage if used unwisely. With a firearm, however, the margin of error is razor-thin.

Shooting a gun isn't something to take lightly. I've been shot at, mistaken for a deer at over three hundred yards (thank God the guy couldn't shoot worth a shit). And my brother-in-law has a sweatshirt with two holes through the hood; he came within two inches of taking a 30-06 slug through the base of the skull. And for every close call, there's another story with a tragic ending.

All you need to remember are a few simple rules to avoid accidents. About 99.8 percent of all firearm accidents could be avoided if the person behind the trigger followed them, and yet they're just commonsense guidelines.

1. Never point your gun in the direction of another person, or where a person could possibly be at any given time.
2. Know your background. Where's the slug going if you miss? Are there houses behind your target? Roads? Livestock?
3. Treat every gun as if it was loaded. It's easy to forget about that one last cartridge.
4. Leave the safety on until the gun is pointed at the target and you're ready to pull the trigger.
5. Put the safety on immediately after you make your shot.

One more thing before I climb back down off my soapbox: Firearms are just flat-out fun, especially when you hit what you're aiming at. The following chapters offer brief summaries on common shooting mistakes and ways to improve your hit rate with a rifle, shotgun, or pistol.

(51) Rifles

There are three basic varieties of rifles commonly available to the American public: semiauto, bolt-action, and lever-action. Semiautos don't require any hand mechanics between shots, as the explosion of one shot ejects the spent shell and replaces it with a fresh cartridge. Bolt-action rifles require the shooter to manually pull back a bolt that ejects the old shell, and a lever-action requires a handle to be worked up and down to replace the cartridge. Bolt-actions are the slowest but most accurate, while semiautos are the fastest and usually shoot the poorest groups. Lever-action rifles fall in the middle ground for both speed and accuracy.

Nestle the butt of the gun snugly into your shoulder. Do not hold it in front of your shoulder in the hope the recoil won't be as bad; the tighter the gun is to your shoulder, the less painful the recoil will be. Held correctly, the recoil won't hurt unless you're shooting large-caliber rifles.

Once you've found your anchor point, steady the front of the barrel by gripping the forestock. This grip is the determining factor for your accuracy, so it's best to rest the forestock against something. Sandbags or a tripod are ideal, but rarely available in the field. Use whatever you can, whether it's a fallen log, fencepost, or mound of earth. Make sure it's solid, and check that the muzzle isn't obstructed. The most accurate shooting position is prone, followed by sitting, kneeling, and finally standing, or freehand.

Shooting: Prone Position. *The only real difficulty in shooting prone is finding an adequate view of your target. Choose your location carefully, avoiding depressions or brushy areas.*

Shooting: Kneeling Position. *Lock your elbow onto the knee for a stable rest when shooting from this position.*

Shooting: Sitting Position. *Lock both elbows into your knees for the most stability when shooting in this position.*

If you're prone, lie flat on your belly and prop your left elbow against the ground, cradling the rifle forestock with your left hand. If you're sitting, rest your right elbow on your right knee, left elbow on the left knee. If you need a little more elevation, go to the kneeling position. Rest your left elbow against the top of your right knee, but be sure to keep your left knee planted firmly on the ground for steadiness.

For true freehand shooting (standing up, nothing to brace against), it's all a matter of muscle control. The important thing here is to not try to hit an exact bull's-eye. Instead, allow the sights to rotate slightly, circling around the bull's-eye, spiraling in tighter and tighter circles until you pull the trigger. To shoot well in the field, you'll have to be good at freehand and sitting/kneeling shooting, since there's often little time to get into a prone position.

The most common reason for missed shots is jerking the trigger. This is a very natural response, a biological imperative of sorts, closely related to the fight-or-flight response. In other words, once we've acquired our target, we just want to get it the hell over with. But pulling hard on the trigger greatly reduces accuracy.

When it comes time to pull the trigger, take a deep breath, and then let it halfway out. As you release the second half of your breath, very slowly apply pressure to the trigger. You should be surprised by the shot. If you think you might be flinching, have a helper load your gun for you, with instructions to give you a blind load at random intervals. If you jump and the only report is a click, you'll know you need to work on your steadiness. Most rifles have adjustable trigger pull tension, which range from about three to ten pounds. Lighter trigger pulls are much easier to shoot.

Shooting well looks deceptively simple, but it takes nerves of steel and years of practice. For most of the population, poor groups aren't due to the gun; almost every decent-quality gun manufactured in the past fifty years can shoot fairly tight groups right out of the box. Instead, it's a matter of keeping the gun steady while you pull the trigger.

 Shotguns

Shotguns come in a whole bunch of models. There are pump-action shotguns (the forestock moves back and forth to eject spent casings and chamber new rounds), semiautos, over-and-unders and side-by-sides (if I have to explain these, you don't deserve to pick up a gun), and single-barrels. They are all designed to shoot hundreds of small pellets in an expanding cone, or pattern, and are rarely effective over fifty or sixty yards. But at close range, say ten yards, they'll blow a basketball-sized hole in any living thing.

The rate at which the cone of shot, or pattern, expands is controlled by the shotgun choke. The choke can sometimes be changed by unscrewing the existing choke (a short metal cylinder) and twisting in a new one. Other shotguns have built-in chokes engineered right into the barrel, which can't be changed. You should be able to tell if you have an interchangeable choke by looking at the end of the barrel. If there's a metal tube with notched ends at the end of the barrel, the choke is interchangeable.

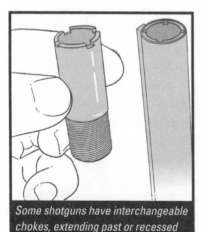

Some shotguns have interchangeable chokes, extending past or recessed inside the muzzle.

It's essential to use the right choke size for the shooting situation. Full chokes expand the least, giving the greatest range but lowest margin for error. An improved cylinder choke expands the most, making it effective for close-quarters wing shooting, but has a limited range. The modified choke lies between the two. There are many other chokes, but those three are the most common.

The mechanics of shooting a shotgun are much different than shooting a rifle. While your target is usually closer and you have a much wider shot pattern (hundreds of BBs versus one slug), the target is also typically more mobile, either running or flying. As such, you'll need to quickly ascertain the speed and direction of your target and shoot in the place where your target *will* be. Not, you'll notice, where it *is*. There's a big difference. To hit moving targets with any degree of consistency, you have to lead your target. There are two basic ways to do this.

First, get your muzzle out ahead of the target, anywhere from six inches to five feet or more, depending on target speed. Press your cheek to the stock, so you're looking down the length of the barrel at the front sight, but don't focus on the front sight—focus on the target beyond it. Many people don't get their cheek down on the stock quickly, and they're so busy trying to acquire the front sight that they never see the target clearly.

Develop your lead, then squeeze the trigger while maintaining the lead. *This means you have to keep your gun moving even as you pull the trigger.* While most people seem to be able to get the hang of leading their target, only a percentage are able to keep their gun moving while they pull the trigger. It's the old walk-and-chew-bubble-gum at the same time dilemma. Nine times out of ten, pass-shooting misses are behind the target.

Another, more natural technique is to swing the end of the shotgun through the target, squeezing the trigger immediately after developing the correct lead. By swinging through your target, the momentum keeps developing your lead even as you pull the trigger.

If you have any doubt about how easy it is to "underlead" a target, try pass-shooting low-flying targets over water some day. You'll be surprised how much lead is required to hit a clay pigeon moving in front of you, and shooting over water shows you exactly where your pellets are going. Even good shooters often miss twenty or thirty feet behind a speedy teal. If in doubt, lead too much: You'll either miss entirely, or hit your target toward the front of the body, which is a lethal shot.

 Pistols

My football coach was fond of hollering three words—well, he was fond of hollering all kinds of words, most of which aren't printable. But the ones I'm referring to here are *north and south*. He liked to preach this tactic for running the ball, with the implication that cutbacks, sweeps, or any way other than right through the other team's teeth was the wrong way. It was okay advice for football, but perfect for shooting a pistol.

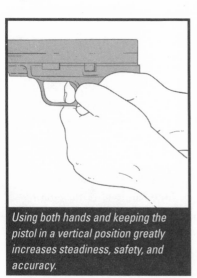

Using both hands and keeping the pistol in a vertical position greatly increases steadiness, safety, and accuracy.

Shooting a pistol while holding it sideways is an excellent way to miss everything you shoot at. The butt of the pistol should be straight down, the top facing straight up. Pistols are hard enough to shoot accurately without trying to show off.

The easiest grip, and one of the most accurate, is the simple two-handed grip. Hold the pistol in your right hand, then overlap your left hand. Tuck your thumbs down, and make sure your fingers in the back are far enough down so the action (on a semiauto) doesn't hit your hand when it slides back during the ejection process. I neglected to do this once, and the pistol tattooed a square into the meaty area at the base of my thumb. I bled all over the place, and it took forever to clean the gun up.

Hold your arms straight out at eye level, feet shoulder-width apart. Line up the front and rear sights, but only the front sight should be sharp. This helps keep the pistol where you want it to be and reduces waggle.

Just like rifle shooting, it's imperative that you pull the trigger smoothly. Don't punch the trigger, or push the gun forward as you shoot. Again, this looks cool when the bad guys do it on television, but it also explains why nobody from the A-team ever took a slug to the chest. Even that little bit of motion is enough to throw the pistol out of line, resulting in a wild shot.

54 Operating Spincast and Baitcast Reels

Of the two common fishing reels, spincast reels are generally easier to operate, especially for lighter tackle. The reel hangs down from the rod, and you reel with your left hand (for right-handed people). To cast this type of reel, hold the line against the base of the rod with your right index finger then flip open the bail with your left hand.

Bring the rod back with your right hand, then bring it forward

Your finger acts as a temporary bail with a spincast reel.

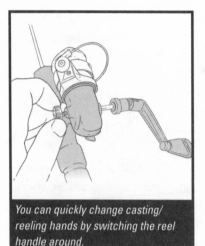

You can quickly change casting/ reeling hands by switching the reel handle around.

and release the line with your finger. Once the lure hits the water, simply flip the bail back over and start reeling. If reeling with your left hand feels too awkward, you can easily switch the handle around so you reel with your dominant hand. Just unscrew the handle, slide it out, and reinsert from the other end. While this makes it easier to reel, it also weakens your hook-setting power, since you're now relying on your nondominant hand for the hook-set.

If you're fishing for a finicky fish with live bait, you can leave the bail open so it can take your offering without feeling resistance. Make sure the line catches in the groove at the base of the bail when you flip it back over. If it doesn't catch, the line will flip the bail back up when you try to set the hook, and you'll end up losing a lot of fish at the side of the boat.

The downside to using a spincast reel is the drag. The drag is the adjustable tension in your reel, used to automatically give line once a certain pressure is attained. Ideally, the drag is set just below the breaking point of your line, which means you can exert the maximum pressure on the fish without breaking the line. With spincast reels, the drag is usually either at the base or top of the reel, making mid-catch adjustments tricky.

Baitcast reels, on the other hand, have an inherently smooth drag, and it's located on the side of the reel for easy adjustment. These attributes make baitcast reels ideal for bigger fish, and are almost always used over spincast reels for big-water sportfishing. Baitcast reels, however, are generally more difficult to cast. The spindle holding the line spins as line goes out, and it doesn't stop when the lure does. It keeps on spinning, and unless you stop it with your thumb, a backlash will result. A backlash resembles a giant bird's nest of tangled line, and generally only happens when the fish are in a feeding frenzy. They take approximately five hours to untangle.

To avoid backlashes, keep the pad of your thumb on the spool as the lure nears the water. Apply pressure just as, or right before, the lure hits the water. This stops the spool from spinning, which in turn prevents that dreaded backlash. Most baitcast reels come with an adjustable spool control, which adjusts the spool spin rate. Imagine this option as a type of parking brake, which can make the spool very resistant to spin or, when set on low, will cause only a slight drag. You'll get better casting distance with less resistance, but will be more prone to backlashes. Just experiment a little to find the right combination for the reel you're using.

Casting a Fly Rod

Okay, okay, I know. You've seen *A River Runs Through It*, you've heard people talk about matching the hatch, you've read pages of purple prose about the mystical transfer of weight as the line unfurls in the early morning mist, and finally you say, ah, the hell with *this*, I'm gonna go buy a dozen worms and a six-pack and sit in my lawn chair by the river until I fall asleep.

Well, both approaches have their merit, but you don't have to commune with nature to throw a fly at a rising fish. All you have to do is know how to get the damn thing out there. And once you manage that, the rest is just plain fun. Besides the obvious thrill of seeing a fish slurp a fly off the surface, fish put up a terrific fight on a fly rod.

A typical dry fly, complete with steel hook, weighs roughly nothing. Most fly-fishing occurs in shallow water, where fish are easily spooked, so you'll need to throw this speck of feathers and thread a considerable distance, sometimes upward of fifty feet. Since the fly weighs next to nothing, you accomplish this by using the weight and momentum of the line, not the lure.

The fly is attached to a leader, typically tapered monofilament six to ten feet long. The leader attaches directly to the fly line, which is weighted. You can use floating or sinking-tip fly line, depending on if you're fishing on the surface or below it, a common way to fish nymphs or streamers. The fly line is attached to backing, or tough braided line that usually remains on the reel.

For the best results, have thirty feet or more of level clearance in front of and behind you. Wading out into a shallow lake is perfect, and catching sunfish and bass is an addictive sport and a great way to start out. It's easiest to cast at a diagonal angle to increase the backcasting

The most common mistake beginning fly anglers make is starting out with too much line. Start out with minimal line until you get the hang of casting longer loops.

area behind you. If you want to practice at home, just stand in your front yard and remove the fly from the end of the leader.

Strip out about six feet of line and hold the excess with your left hand. You can strip out more line and let it pool in front of you, but you'll be more prone to tangles. Hold the rod in your right hand, and use your index finger to hold the line just above the reel. Grip the excess line in your left hand, then lift the tip of the fly rod up so the weighted line is just off the water. Now you're ready for your first cast.

Move your arm back to the two o'clock position, lifting the flyline off the water, while still holding the excess line in your other hand. As the line unfurls behind you, you'll feel the weight of the line going back. Right before it stops, simply move your arm forward to the ten o'clock position, which will propel the line forward. Try to keep your elbow level, like it's sliding along a shelf. Once the line straightens out in front of you, let out some of the excess line and lower your rod tip. The line should set down gently on the water.

Since most fly rods are seven to nine feet long, with a similar length of leader material, this means your fly is now roughly twenty to twenty-five feet in front of you. This is plenty for most fishing, and there's no need for false casting (repeated passes of the fly line to build up distance).

If you do need to go farther, don't set the rod tip down. Instead, wait until the line unfurls in front of you and then draw it back again, stripping more line off the reel with your left hand and feeding the slack into the back loop. Repeat this process until you're out far enough or you get tangled up, whichever comes first. Be warned, though—repeat this more than three or four times, and the line gets difficult to handle. Don't false cast just because you think it looks cool; remember, a river might run through it, but enough false casts and an alder bush *will* snag it.

If you're casting in running water, cast slightly upstream of the area where the fish are rising. Be sure to lift the rod tip as the fly drifts downstream, which prevents the line from bellying and creating an unnatural drag on the fly. Be sure to keep the slack at a minimum, since a quick hook-set is essential. Many fish will spit a fly back out once they realize it tastes like feathers and glue.

There's no need to stick with dry flies, either. Nymphs, an imitation of a larval insect, are deadly on stream fish. Streamers, which mimic swimming invertebrates or small minnows, can be cast out and slowly reeled back in by hand-stripping. Whatever you use, be sure to run it by you on the water a few times to get an idea of how it looks and moves in the water. If it looks unnatural, switch flies or retie the knot. If you stick with it, you'll soon discover that flies or streamers can often outfish that gob of crawlers.

It's a little harder to drink that six-pack between bites, though.

Tying a Fishing Knot

Every year I lose at least a couple of big fish because of a bad fishing knot. Well, I think they were big. I know it's not much of a story when the one that got away was a half-pound perch.

Regardless of the size of the fish, the knot is the weakest point of any fishing system, and a poor knot all but eliminates your chances of catching a trophy.

There are at least a dozen good formulas for making a fishing knot, most of which involve detailed diagrams and will leave your basic engineer scratching his head. These knots are strong, with great names like the Bimini Twist and the Palomar. They are also inevitably forgotten when the fish are biting on your buddy's side of the boat and you need to change lures in a hurry.

You really only need one good knot, and the improved clinch knot, or the fisherman's knot, is a quick, strong knot that lends itself well to trolling, jigging, or fly-fishing. It's also about the simplest knot, other than your basic double granny, and double grannies don't work. Trust me on this one.

Thread about four inches of line through the eye, double it back, and pinch it between your thumb and index finger. Now twist the line between your fingers until the two sections of line are wrapped completely around each other, then thread the free end into the loop of line just above the hook eye. Pull the loose end down while pulling up a little on the other section of line, then take the loose end and slide it back through the top loop. Keeping upward pressure on the free end, slide the hook downward until it's snug, and trim the excess line.

If you're trolling or casting a minnow imitation, make sure the knot is in line with the rest of the lure and not cocked to one side or the other. This keeps the lure running in a straight line. If it's crooked, just pull it straight or tweak carefully with needle-nose pliers.

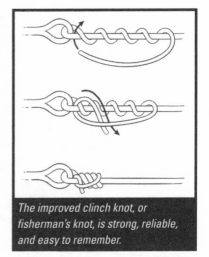

The improved clinch knot, or fisherman's knot, is strong, reliable, and easy to remember.

57) Removing a Fish Hook from Your Body

It was a beautiful spring day, just right for two of my favorite pastimes. I hopped on my motorcycle, loaded my fishing gear into my backpack, and headed down to the river. The fishing hole was unoccupied, and I quickly parked my bike and assembled my rod.

There was only one problem: My favorite lure, a minnow imitation with several treble hooks, had worked free of my tacklebox and the hooks were embedded deep in the nylon stitching of my backpack. I was too impatient to cut them out, so I just grabbed hold of the lure with my pliers and gave a good yank. In a split-second I had removed all the hooks from my backpack . . . and embedded them squarely into the meaty part of my thumb.

After I got done swearing, I took a look at my hand. The hooks were relatively small, which meant I couldn't push them out and clip the barb even if I wanted to—and I didn't want to. I wanted Novocain and a sympathetic nurse, so I hopped back on my bike to catch a ride to the hospital.

You know, it hurts when you stick a barbed hook into your thumb. Hurts pretty bad. Not quite as bad as driving three miles home on a motorcycle, a minnow-shaped piece of balsa wood flapping in the wind. Nor is the pain purely physical. If you doubt this, try sitting in the waiting room of an ER for a half hour with a fake rainbow chub hanging from your hand.

Removing a hook yourself is cheaper and faster than going to a doctor, and it's a lot less embarrassing, too. It also hurts like hell, but if you're deep in the wilderness and far from a doctor, it's usually less painful to remove it yourself than wait for the floatplane.

Pulling a barbed hook out the way it went in is incredibly tough, hurts very badly, and can cause a lot of bleeding. A much better way is to push the hook out, snip off the barb, and retract it. This is easier with bigger hooks, since they have a larger bend and are consequently easier to turn back out through the skin. If the hook is attached to a lure with more than one set of hooks, be sure to remove the extra set of hooks first. It's all too easy to double—or treble—your trouble when the twitching and the swearing starts in earnest.

Let it bleed for at least a minute after you pull the hook out. Puncture wounds are notoriously prone to infection, and blood naturally rinses the hole, removing rust and bacteria present on the hook. Then bandage it up and go stagger back into the tent to sleep it off.

What—you didn't just pull that out while you were *sober*, did you?

General Motor Boat Operation

Man, was I jealous.

I was stuck in my senior year of college, barely able to afford a used canoe. But my buddy had gotten a decent job right out of high school, and on this warm June day we were jetting around in his brand new aluminum fishing boat, complete with a big and shiny outboard motor, making a pretense of fishing while we checked out the local sunbathing scenes.

My buddy had to work in the afternoon, but we screwed around out on the lake until the last possible minute. Then, heedless of breaking the motor in—or the large rocks lurking under the surface—we cruised in to the landing at roughly fifty miles per hour.

"Hey, you gonna slow down?" I asked as we rapidly approached the dock.

My buddy smiled cockily. "We'll be all right." It was his first boat, but I'm pretty sure he was imagining himself with gold captain's bars already. He didn't stay cocky for long; even after he cut the motor, it was obvious we were going to reach the dock at much too high of a speed. He yelled at our other friend, a beefy guy with arms as big around as my thighs, to grab the dock.

Well, ole Beefcake managed to grab the dock, but he was no match for over a thousand pounds of momentum. The aluminum hull crashed into the wooden dock at about ten miles an hour and crumpled like an empty beer can. Suddenly, what had been a sleek, wedge-shaped bullet was transformed into something that resembled one of the amphibious landers on Normandy Beach.

It was a beautiful day, and the sunbathing scene was pretty spectacular, but suddenly we were the main attraction.

My buddy learned one very important thing that day: Boats don't have brakes. Many models have steering wheels, and a dashboard that resembles a car, but the similarities with an automobile pretty much end there. Whether you're planning on purchasing a new boat or simply renting one for some weekend fun, beginning boaters often encounter quite a few operational, mechanical, and judgmental quandaries. Here are some of the most common problems.

Starting and Running an Outboard Motor

Starting the engine seems pretty simple, and many times it's simply a matter of turning the key. But if nothing happens, you might not have a dead battery. All outboard and inboard engines won't start if the gear shifter isn't in neutral—a standard safety precaution. Check to make sure you're in neutral, then try it again.

If the battery is dead, you can try to get a jump start from another boat. However, many fishing boats also have a separate trolling motor battery, also called a deep-cycle battery, which can be used to start the motor. Switch the starting battery back once the boat starts. Just don't touch the cables together when you're switching them, and don't shut the motor off for at least fifteen minutes, which should be enough time for the alternator to charge up the dead battery. In a pinch, you can also disconnect the battery from your truck in lieu of an extra trolling motor battery. Just don't run the truck battery down, too, unless your boating plans call for an excursion up that old and fabled creek.

Many smaller outboards can be started manually with a pull rope (in fact, this is the only option for starting some motors). If there isn't one on the motor, just pop the motor cover off—you'll see the flywheel right on top. Wind the rope (if there isn't an emergency pull rope in the boat, a shoelace sometimes works) around the groove in the flywheel, then yank on it.

If the battery is cranking over fine, but the motor still won't start, squeeze the fuel bulb a few times to make sure you're getting gas into the carburetor. The fuel bulb is located along the fuel line, usually fairly close to the motor. Squeeze it until it gets hard (get your mind out of the gutter), then try it again.

If it's cold out, or if the motor has sat for a while, you'll need to choke the motor. Start out with full choke, but be prepared to quickly shut it down to half-choke; outboards tend to rev extremely high on full choke. If the boat has a hand throttle lever, there's often a button on the pivot point of the throttle lever. Press this button to bring the throttle level forward without engaging the transmission; this means you can rev up the motor without putting it in gear. Just bring the throttle lever back to neutral after the motor is warm. You'll hear a click, which means you can engage the transmission.

Heading Out to Sea

Once you've got the motor started, make sure you cast off any lines holding you to the dock and/or pull up the anchor. Don't accelerate rapidly at landing areas; docking and trailering boats can be a delicate task, and excessive wakes are a pain for other boaters trying to get in or out of the water.

Getting on plane is a term that refers to running your boat on the same horizontal plane as the water surface. You'll have to attain a certain speed to "plane out," but the exact speed depends on boat shape, size, and load. You'll want to get up on plane if you're going long distances; running in the diagonal "bow up" half speed is inefficient and danger-ous in big waves, even if you're going slower than you would on plane.

Make sure the motor is in the full-down position. There's usually a thumb lever on the side of the throttle lever on console-driven boats, which is called the tilt-and-trim button. Tilt and trim are actually the same thing—*tilt* usually refers to changing motor angles at rest, and *trim* refers to changing motor angles while on plane.

Many tiller-operated boats (no steering wheel) have a lever at the base of the motor for adjusting the height of the propeller. You can lock the motor in the down position or halfway up—you won't have the full range of positions that automatic (battery-operated) tilt-and-trim motors have. However, one nice option on tiller-operated boats is a release tilt, which lets the motor swing freely if you hit a submerged rock or log.

Once you've got the motor all the way down, accelerate smoothly. The front of the boat will begin to rise, which is normal. Just keep accelerating until the front of the boat comes back down. Now you're on plane, and probably moving fairly quickly across the top of the water. If you have power trim, slowly begin to raise the motor back up. This, in turn, raises the bow (front) of the boat back up. You'll get an increase in speed and fuel efficiency on a properly trimmed boat, because you won't be plowing through as much water. Learning when to stop raising the motor is dependent on boat style and load, but you can usually hear the motor smooth out when you hit the sweet spot. Just don't raise the motor so much that the prop comes out of the water.

If you encounter big waves, it is imperative to keep the bow pointed into them, either straight on or at a quartering angle. This might mean making a long detour at two oblique angles, but one of the main causes of capsizing is maintaining a course where waves can slam into the side of the boat. Bows are made to handle waves, not sterns or gunwales (backs or sides, respectively)—that's why they're pointed.

Heading In from Sea

As the story of my friend's new boat demonstrates, boats do not have brakes. Putting the motor in neutral only slows you down—and killing the motor is the worst thing you can do; if the motor is running you can at least use the reverse gear to stop or slow your forward progress. At higher speeds, turning works much better than slowing or stopping when you need to avoid an obstacle.

Maneuvering the boat at slower speeds can actually be more difficult than at higher speeds. Unlike a car, you don't have any friction between your vehicle and the driving surface to make tight turns. The best philosophy is a simple one: Move in a predetermined, straight line. This is actually faster than zooming in, reversing, and making frantic adjustments.

Standard Boat Maintenance and Equipment

Many outboard motors still operate on two-cycle technology. This means a certain amount of oil is mixed right into the gasoline. Depending on the make and model, you may have to mix the gas yourself (usually fifty parts gas to one part two-cycle oil), or you may have to fill up an oil reservoir (oil-injected models). Make sure you know the right way to fuel up—adding the wrong fuel mixture is an easy way to ruin an expensive boat motor.

Like a lot of small engines, it's not a good idea to use ethanol blends in your boat motor. This type of fuel can gum up your carburetor pretty quickly. And when you're on the water, a stalled outboard motor is a bit more serious than having a breakdown on the shoulder of a highway with your car.

Many boats don't come equipped with what veteran sailors would consider essential boat equipment. Just as you wouldn't embark on a long road trip without a good spare tire, neither should you head out on the water without some standard boat equipment and some quick-fix knowledge.

- **Boat plug.** Yeah, this is a pretty essential piece of equipment. Make sure it's in place before you drop the boat into the water. Forgetting this happens to thousands of boaters every year, even experienced ones. Not me, of course. Never happened, I tell you. Never.

- **Bilge pump.** This is a submersible pump located in the hull of the boat that pumps water back into the sea. Use it if you're taking on water from a leak, big waves, or a heavy rainstorm. Just leave it on until you're in the clear; most bilge pumps have a float switch that shuts them off when water levels decrease. If you have a bilge pump, check to make sure it's operational by lifting the float switch before you hit big water.
- **Water intake.** If you run your boat prop through heavy weeds or drag the propeller through a sandbar, the intake can plug up. This will cause the motor to overheat in short order. Turn the engine off and tilt the motor all the way; you'll see a screen just above the propeller, on the side of the shaft. Clean the screen out and lower the motor back into the water. Water should spit out the port just under the motor, above the waterline. If not, you may need to replace the impeller, a small in-line pump that circulates cooling water through the boat engine. This isn't an on-the-water repair job. Limp it home and replace the impeller before you go back out.
- **Anchor.** Every boat should have an anchor and at least 100 feet of rope, even if you're not planning on stopping. If your motor stalls and it's a windy day, a good anchor can keep you off the rocks until help arrives or you fix the problem.

59 Canoe Basics

The only way to stay inside a canoe for any length of time is to remain in the center, keep your body as low as possible, and avoid sudden side-to-side movements. This means you have to stay seated, and you can't lean over the side of the canoe to net a fish, spit tobacco, or look at your reflection. I've been in tip-overs with people who have done all of 'em, and I've been guilty a time or two myself.

When you step into or out of a canoe, be sure to step exactly in the middle, and have the other person steady the canoe until you're seated. If it's too shallow to load from the side, load the back of the canoe into the water first, leaving the bow resting lightly on the bank. Have one person steady the canoe while the stern paddler gets seated. Once the stern paddler is seated, he should wedge his paddles into the lake bottom to steady the canoe while the bow paddler gets in. Then gently rock the canoe back into the water.

When exiting, have the person in the bow get out first, while the person in the stern again uses both paddles to steady the canoe. Again, run the bow up on land if possible, which will stabilize the canoe.

Canoes can handle surprisingly big waves, but only with experienced paddlers inside and *only* when the canoe is running with the waves. Sometimes this means a long detour at right angles to the point you're trying to reach and a lot of hard paddling, but it's still faster than swimming. Trying to take even small waves at cross angles can mean a quick dunking.

Keep all your gear in waterproof containers, since very few canoes arrive at their destination without some water being dripped into the bottom. Even the simple act of switching sides with the paddle can accumulate a lot of water in the bottom of the canoe. A couple of strips of lightweight wood underneath your gear works great to keep everything off the wet bottom, and oversized garbage bags make great temporary rain jackets for your gear.

Solo paddling is tough, since even a light wind will push the bow around, making it difficult to steer. If you have to paddle alone, place some weight in the front of the canoe. Lacking actual gear, I've used large rocks and, on one memorable occasion, a keg of beer to balance out the load. Don't worry about the extra weight; a heavier, well-balanced canoe is far easier to navigate than a light, back-heavy one.

Running Rapids

Rapids — those frothy, treacherous, often boulder-filled stretches of fast water—are a major part of what canoeing is all about. They can also wreck a canoe in seconds. The key to staying dry and having fun is planning out your route through the rapids beforehand. For bigger rapids, or long runs, beach the canoe upstream, then walk downstream to get an idea of where your best route lies.

That said, very few preplanned routes go exactly as planned. "Stay-the-course" is not an option, and missing one arc of your route can mean all subsequent plans are suddenly useless. When you do stray from the planned course, it's essential that you communicate clearly with your partner. Usually, the person in the bow will call the shots, while the person in back supplies most of the steering power. It's essential that both of you know what it means when the bow yells "Right!" Does it mean there's a rock on the right, or does it mean go right? Confusion results in midstream pirouettes, tip-overs, and smashed canoes.

You can usually mark submerged rocks by their boils. If the boil is frothy, the rock is usually just underneath the surface. Deeper rocks will usually have smoother boils, though sometimes a flat-topped rock just underneath the surface will have a smooth boil. The deepest water is also usually where the fastest current flows, so following the main runs generally equals the smoothest ride.

If you do get hung up on a rock, it's almost impossible to push the canoe back upstream to free yourself. Instead, push off to one side, being careful to avoid a sideways flip. If you push far enough out into the current, the water will often grab the canoe and swing you off the rock. Unfortunately, this also means you might end up running the rapids backward. On the upside, you get to see a lot of amused faces from the paddlers behind you as you try to get turned back around.

61 Portaging

Faced with a dangerous set of rapids or a strip of land separating two lakes, many canoers will hop out and carry their gear overland. This isn't an overly technical process, but there are a few tips that will make the land journey a little less brutal.

The easiest way to haul a canoe is to invert it over your head and start walking (actually, the easiest way is getting your partner to carry it). This is called portaging, and it sucks. There are a couple of tricks to make it suck less, though.

For a standard grip, stand halfway down the length of the canoe, then lift and flip it over your shoulders in one smooth movement. Set the center rib on the canoe across your shoulders, grab hold of the far end of each rib ahead of you, and tilt the canoe up slightly so you can see where you're going. Pad the rib with an old shirt or piece of foam before you start out. Once you get the canoe up on your shoulders you'll want to keep it there, as it takes more energy to set it down and pick it back up than it does to keep walking.

The major issue here is balance. Historically, many Native Americans used a tump, or a strap of leather that loops over the forehead and connects to the center ribs (one rib back from the ones you'd normally hang onto with your hands). This practice, which continues today with many serious canoers, directs the canoe weight to the center of your back and frees your hands, reducing arm fatigue. If your canoe wants to tip forward or backward, you can adjust the tump length or add a piece of gear to the front or back of the canoe. Canoes aren't heavy, just awkward, and tumps work great for easing your overland journeys.

Telling Direction with a Compass

Well, this is easy enough, right? Hold the compass out flat on your palm, far away from any magnetic fields that might cause interference, like batteries or power lines. Then tap it once or twice and wait until the needle swings north. Rotate the compass so that the needle lines up with the north direction, and you know all four directions.

Yeah, but where the hell are you? And in which of the four clearly defined directions do you go?

Too many people venture into the woods with a compass and figure they can't get lost. The problem is, they don't have any idea of where they are (they're lost, duh) because they never took a reading before they headed into the woods. They might know where north and south are, but that doesn't help one single bit. About the best a compass can do now is keep them from walking in circles.

A compass is an invaluable tool for navigating through unfamiliar territory, but it needs to be used *before* you get lost. Use your compass like joggers use a watch, checking in periodically to track your progress. Ascertaining your line of travel isn't just a matter of looking at the needle, though. You need to pick out landmarks in front of and behind your current location. This will allow you to visually draw a line of travel, which you can use to determine the direction that will lead you out of the woods. It is essential to do this frequently so you have a continuous line of landmarks to follow and reference. Coupled with frequent compass checks, it's almost impossible to get lost this way.

If the land is flat and/or heavily wooded, you'll need to stop more often than in hilly or open regions, since landmarks won't be visible for extended periods. Regardless of the terrain, pay attention to the surrounding countryside by designating certain trees, hills, or boulders as landmarks. Take a moment to memorize each one. This keeps you moving in a straight line, and familiarizes you with each area you pass through. If you still get turned around, the odds of finding a familiar sight increase exponentially.

A map, even a cheap roadmap, can work wonders in conjunction with a compass. Again, determine your line of travel before you start, find a couple of landmarks in the distance (even if it's not in the direction you want to go), and mark them on the map. Keep doing this, and odds are you can easily look around at any time and know your general location.

Telling Direction Without a Compass

There are many different ways to tell directions without a compass, all with varying degrees of accuracy. The most consistent markers are the celestial objects, such as the sun and stars. The rising or setting sun is pretty much a no-brainer, but it can be difficult to tell which direction it's heading in the middle of the day or behind heavy clouds. And if you're lost, waiting a couple of hours for the sunset can be excruciating.

If there's enough light to cast a shadow, find an open area and drive a big stick into the ground. Then use another stick to mark the line of the shadow. Wait about fifteen minutes, then mark the new line with another stick, approximately half of the way up the shadow. Draw a line between these two sticks for an approximate east-west line.

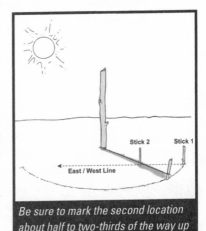

Be sure to mark the second location about half to two-thirds of the way up the shadow line for an approximate east-west line.

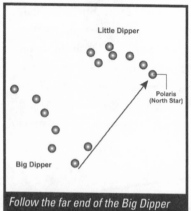

Follow the far end of the Big Dipper up four times the depth of the dipper. The North Star is the brightest star in the localized region.

At night, the easiest way to find north is to look for Polaris, or the North Star. This isn't nearly as tough as it might seem, because all you have to do is locate the Big Dipper. Extend an imaginary line from the end of the dipper, about four times the depth of the dipper, to find Polaris. Since it might be hard to remember where north was when daylight comes, line Polaris up with a prominent landmark (e.g., a tall tree or hill), then mark the spot where you're standing. If you can't find a recognizable landmark in the starlight, mark one area on the ground with a stick or rock, then back up about twenty feet, all the while keeping Polaris directly in front of you. Draw a line between your two marks in the morning, and you'll know your north-south line.

A waxing or waning moon is also a great way to tell direction. If the moon rises before sunset, the illuminated side is west. If the moonrise occurs after midnight, the illuminated side is to the east.

Once you look down on the ground, things get iffy in a hurry. Moss will grow around the entire base of the tree, but will usually be thickest on the north side. Tree branches will be fewer and sparser on the north side, and animals tend to build nests and dens in areas with maximum sunlight exposure, such as south-facing slopes. These clues should be good enough to give you a rough estimate of the direction you need to travel, but are by no means infallible. Never rely on one clue; instead, use a weight-of-evidence approach.

If you end up lost—and let's face it, if you're inspecting moss depth on tree trunks you're freaking lost—you *have* to make yourself sit down and relax. In fact, it's usually best to remain right there, since wandering off is the most dangerous thing you can do. Odds are you'll be found in short order.

But if you're deep in the woods and nobody's looking for you, it's essential that you keep walking in a straight line, using whatever directions you can gather from your surroundings. Eventually you'll hit a road or a stream, either of which will eventually lead you to civilization.

64 Understanding and Working with Dogs

Aggressive and uncooperative dogs are just a plain old headache. Yet almost every dog can be a useful, devoted pet. The key to turning Cujo into Lassie involves a simple attitude adjustment—and not just for the dog.

Dogs are pack animals. While many people understand this, they can't seem to grasp another concept: Unless you establish dominance over a dog, you are not a respected member of its pack. You are competition, and unless you want to spend the next ten to fifteen years of your life lying belly-up every time Fido comes over, you're going to have a bad relationship with your dog. The key task in forming a successful relationship with any dog is to put it at ease, which essentially means making it feel like it's in a pack situation. If you're the owner, this means establishing a hierarchy, with you at the top.

No matter how much you love your dog, you must be the pack leader, the alpha male or alpha female. This doesn't mean you should beat your dog and then go pee on the corner of his doghouse. It simply means that you have to make the dog respect you by dispensing justice in a fair, consistent manner. No need to beat him, but no slacking off, either. Dogs need discipline to function within a family unit. This means not letting them run in the house before you, making sure they listen to you all the time, and setting consequences for bad behavior. Consistently. It's work, just like parenting, but if you do it correctly, and at an early age, you'll never be one of those sorry schmucks on a dog version of *Super Nanny*.

Unlike children, dogs lack a highly developed sense of emotional remorse. And, while they understand tone and simple words, lengthy discussions about their bad behavior don't accomplish much. As such, I usually leave the "I'm so disappointed in you" speech at home. Instead, a couple of *moderate* smacks across the shoulder or rump usually get, and hold, their attention. Just to be clear: I've always had Labrador retrievers, big, strong animals who are immune to minor physical discomfort and have the learning curve of a stump. For a high-strung setter or spaniel, or a smaller dog, a swat across the shoulders might not be a good idea. It all depends on the individual dog's temperament, size, and age. Avoid using physical punishment on puppies, too, since you don't want to make your dog overly submissive. These pups can turn out like the canine equivalent of the needy kid at school who always asked where the party was going to be, starting on Tuesday morning.

Treats can be administered for positive behavior, either food snacks or petting, but don't overdo it. You didn't see Mickey giving Rocky a hug every time he landed a jab, didja? No, he just kept working on him to get better, with encouragement added only when he needed it. Save those hugs and kisses for the couch, *after* the training session.

Again, consistency is the key, especially when the dog is young. It sets limits for the dog, and, if done during puppyhood, the dog will rarely, if ever, cross those interior boundaries. Dogs can live ten to fifteen years and are a serious financial and emotional investment. Make sure you spend lots of extra time with them that first couple of years, setting limits, getting the dog to accept its beta role within the household, and basically nipping bad behavior in the bud. It takes work, but the end result is what every dog owner wants: a good dog.

65 Riding a Horse

The most important lesson is simple: Take your wallet out of your pocket. I once rode a horse for an afternoon with my billfold in my back pocket, and then lurched around like Igor the next day, rubbing my butt and vowing I would never ride another horse until all the world's oil was burned up and internal combustion engines were museum pieces.

But I soon forgot about the pain, and now I can look out my window and see dozens of horses grazing in my field. They're the neighbor's horses that broke through the fence and are eating up my hay, true, but I've come to appreciate the uniqueness and usefulness of the equine race. And riding a horse remains about the best way to travel through rough countryside this side of a Humvee.

To most weekend riders, the underlying concern is not getting bucked off. The easiest and simplest way to avoid getting bucked is to pick out a horse with a good disposition. If you have a choice of mounts, pick a horse that will approach you readily, ears up, and sniff at your outstretched hands. A horse that will drop its neck while you're next to it is almost always submissive. Avoid standoffish horses, especially ones that lay their ears back or roll their eyes. These are the horses that are going to make you look like an ass, and usually fairly early in the day. So pick out a nice horse, and then take a few minutes letting it get accustomed to your smell and your actions.

You usually mount the horse from its left side. Slide your left foot into the stirrup, grab the pommel with both hands, and swing your right leg up and over the saddle. Don't hop to get to the stirrups; the stirrup length is easily adjusted by sliding the strap through the circle clasp. Hopping excites the horse and makes you look silly—not a good combination.

Horses respond to pressure, whether it's applied to their sides or head/neck area. You need to apply this pressure through your legs or through the reins, but many beginners apply too much force, resulting in what seems like unpredictable horse behavior. In reality, you're the one who's being unruly. Most riding horses are trained to respond to fairly subtle pressures, and strong yanks and kicks just get them worked up. Apply pressure lightly, either with the reins or your legs. If the horse doesn't respond, let off and then add a little more pressure, but move up gradually. Remember, the horse weighs a thousand pounds more than you; you're *asking* it to move, not telling it.

Trotting, loping, and galloping can be brutal on the inexperienced rider. Instead of bouncing up and down on the saddle (which also bothers the horse), stand up in the saddle, which takes the pressure off your butt and the horse's butt. This will allow you to bounce in rhythm with the horse's gait. It might tire your legs, but it's easier on you both.

Pull back on the reins to get the horse to stop, making sure the muzzle goes down, but don't apply too much force. Forcing the horse's muzzle down too hard will sometimes result in bucking, or a sudden stop that will send you flying over the handlebars.

Transplanting Trees and Shrubs

Yards worldwide are covered with dead and dying transplanted trees. There are usually only two living things involved in the transplant: the tree and the guy who planted it. Guess who's to blame?

The number one cause of transplant death is dehydration. Every time a root is exposed to air, cells begin to die. This severely affects the tree's ability to absorb water, and a cut or broken root exacerbates the problem. And while small roots may seem unimportant, they often have more surface area than the larger roots, which lack the numerous root tendrils essential for water and nutrient uptake. A successful transplant, then, means minimizing damage to the entire root system. This is accomplished by keeping the roots damp and protected.

While most purchased trees and shrubs have their root system in pretty good shape, hand-dug transplants are often DOA, even if they look fine for a few days. The reason these trees don't survive is because their root system has been severed too close to the trunk, with the smaller but essential roots cut away. The circle of sod from a dug transplant should be at least equal to the diameter of the tree's canopy. If you're digging up a sapling with vertically oriented branches, carefully bend one of the main limbs to the side to get an idea of where the root system ends. Digging up this much sod limits your ability to transplant big trees, of course.

Mark the north side of the tree with a piece of tape or a plastic tie before you lift it out of the ground. When you drop it into the new hole, make sure that part of the tree faces north again. Trees often have different morphology on their sunny and shade sides, and switching exposure causes unnecessary stress.

The new hole should be a few inches wider than the tree's base of roots, since cramming a tree in a small hole will cause the root ends to point up or break, reducing water uptake. If the soil is hard, use a shovel or rake to loosen the soil at the bottom of the hole, then dump a bucket of water over the freshly turned soil. This will provide a soft, damp bed for the roots to thread into those crucial first weeks. A layer of wetted potting soil can be substituted, and also provides extra nutrients.

Make sure you fill any gaps with soil and loose strips of sod to retain moisture. It is nearly impossible to overwater a shrub or tree during those first few weeks; it is woefully easy to underwater them. Many people don't realize how much water it takes to soak through to the root system, nor do they realize how quickly loose soil can dry out. Remember, the transplanted roots are functioning very inefficiently at first, and they need to be surrounded by wet soil constantly for the tree to live.

The need for water will remain constant for about a year. While daily waterings aren't necessary after the first few weeks, transplanted trees can't handle long periods of dry weather until the root system is fully developed. Water accordingly.

 ## **Tree Grafting**

I distinctly remember being amazed when I first learned that every single Granny Smith apple originally came from a single tree. The same goes for Honey Crisps, Golden Delicious, and basically every other tree fruit you can find at the grocery store. You can't pop the seeds out of that crispy apple and stick them in a pot, since apple trees cross-pollinate with other apple trees, even if they're crabapples. The resulting offspring will usually produce apples quite unlike their parent stock and are usually inedible. In fact, the odds of finding an edible—not tasty, just edible—apple from a seed is somewhere around a thousand to one.

That's right: Johnny Appleseed was full of shit.

Instead of relying on those odds, the earliest fruit growers started grafting trees to produce clones of the mother tree. To do this, you cut a branch, commonly called a scion, from the parent tree and join it to a root from another strain of tree (from the same species). In fact, almost every fruit tree you see is actually two trees; from the ground up it's the tasty fruit-bearing strain, and underground it's a hardy, disease-resistant rootstock. If you look closely, you can usually see a slight bend or twist in the trunk of any fruit tree, just above the ground. This is where the two sections were joined. Grafting a tree allows you to maintain a desirable line, or even develop your own strain of fruit. It's also much cheaper than buying trees from the nursery.

Start about six to eight weeks before the growing season by ordering a good, hardy rootstock via any tree nursery catalog. You can also buy the branch, or scion, or snip some from the trees you already have. It should be a young scion, with four buds or less, and harvested during winter.

The rootstock and the scion should be about the same diameter. You'll also need a sharp knife, masking or electrical tape, and paraffin wax.

The method I most commonly use is the whip graft. To do this, you cut the rootstock and the scion at about a thirty-degree angle. Use a very sharp knife (dull ones crush the delicate cambium layer) and make an angled cut in one smooth motion through the rootstock. Then cut straight down through the middle of the angle, about as deep as the knife blade. Repeat this on the scion, again cutting fast and

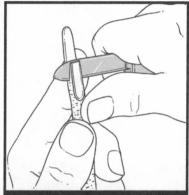

Make complementary diagonal cuts on both the root and scion with a sharp knife. Dull blades crush the delicate cambium layer.

clean through the tissue at the same angle, then notching it longitudinally in the center. Quickly snug the two pieces together to prevent cell damage. It's important that the rootstock and scion match diameter and angle to get the best seal.

Now wrap the two sections together with electrical or masking tape or an asphalt/water emulsion glue, commonly sold at landscaping stores and nurseries. If you use tape, wrap it securely, but don't apply too much pressure. Just like overtightening a tourniquet, applying too much pressure will cut off the life-giving liquid (sap instead of blood). Apply some paraffin wax over the tape to prevent dehydration and disease.

Wrap with damp paper toweling, then damp newspaper, and finally a layer of dry newspaper. Then refrigerate. Leave the grafts alone for six to eight weeks in the fridge, watering occasionally to keep the roots damp. Once you see the root formation poke out, go ahead and plant the tree. Be extremely diligent with your watering schedule. Your success rate is not going to be 100 percent, so you'll want to do this in batches of at least ten.

SECTION 4

Household and Garage

Soldering Copper Pipes

"Ten minutes," I told my wife, heading down to the basement with my plumbing toolbox. Our old water heater had basically disintegrated, but I figured I could install the new one with a few simple twists of a wrench. Upon further inspection, I saw that the new water heater was taller than the old one; I was going to have to cut the pipes and resolder the old fittings onto the cut pipes. Not a problem, I figured, breaking out the torch. Just a walk in the park.

Well, kinda. Four hours later my basement looked like something you'd see driving through Yellowstone Park. Little geysers of water hissed out at unpredictable intervals, pools of cold, clear water dotted the floor, and the guy hunched in the corner bore more than a passing resemblance to a pissed-off grizzly bear.

Soldering copper pipes is actually very easy—if you do it in a dry system. The problem I faced when connecting my new water heater was simple: I was working in a closed plumbing system. Water pipes retain drops of water even after you shut off the main valve, and when you apply heat during soldering, that water turns into steam. Steam builds up pressure in the pipes, which then blows the solder back out the seal, and you end up with water leaks. Little, tiny, infuriating leaks.

If you're working in a closed system—and you probably will be—first shut off the main water valve, then open up every faucet in the house so the steam can dissipate. Some people even shove hunks of white bread inside the pipe before soldering wet lines; the bread soaks up the water, reducing steam (the bread dissolves once the water is turned back on). This has a moderate success rate, since the bread is damp and still produces some steam. Better to just open up faucets and heat the pipe with a propane torch until the steam disappears.

You'll need a pipe cutter, torch, solder, flux, and sandpaper to make a good soldered seal. All are available at home centers for minimal prices, with the torch costing $10–$20. The pipe cutter has to be sharp, since dull cutters often warp the pipe, which in turn forms an imperfect seal with the fitting. Torch gas can be either regular propane or MAPP gas, which is more expensive but burns hotter. If you're using old flux, make sure it isn't lead-based, since this can cause water contamination. All modern flux is lead-free.

Use a rotary pipe cutter to cut the pipe. You can also use a hacksaw, but the cut won't be as smooth. Once you've cut through the pipe, sand the end with sandpaper. This removes burrs and increases surface area, which helps the solder attach to the pipe and connection.

Apply flux to the end of the pipe(s) using a small brush. Flux is an acidic paste that cleans and primes the copper prior to soldering, and it should not be applied with your finger. I once lost my brush while plumbing my house and used my finger instead; after a day or so my finger had swollen so much that it looked like one of those sporting event "We're #1" gloves.

Once the pipe is cut, sanded, and fluxed, insert the fitting. You may have to use a slip coupling if you can't fit a new fitting into the rigid plumbing system (these look the same as regular coupling but don't have interior stops).

Unroll the flux, light your torch, and heat up the fitting. The hottest part of the flame will be right at the end of the blue cone. Heat the middle of the fitting, not the actual seam. Done correctly, the solder will flow toward the hottest part and suck into the fitting. You can almost always tell if you've formed a watertight seal, since the solder will circle the pipe and virtually disappear once you touch it to the seam. If it doesn't, keep heating the fitting. You'll know you're hot enough when the solder is sucked right off the tip.

Gluing PVC and CPVC Pipes

Like copper pipe repairs, the worst enemy when repairing plastic water supply lines is the residual water inside the old pipes. PVC pipe is commonly used for drain lines, and comes in common diameters of 1½ to 4 inches; CPVC plastic pipe is usually used for water supply lines and is usually ½ to 1 inch. Remember, almost all plumbing diameters are identified by I.D., or inside diameter, regardless of outside diameter.

Make sure the fitting and the end of the pipe are clean and dry, then remove any plastic burrs left over from the cutting process. Apply a primer, allow it to dry, and coat both the outside of the pipe and the inside of the fitting with plastic cement. You'll have to move quickly once you apply the cement, as it dries quickly.

Since it's easy to get confused or flustered while connecting pipe quickly, fit everything together first without the glue, mark the fitting and pipe with a permanent marker, then take everything apart, prime it, and glue it back together one piece at a time, matching up your marks. Hold the pieces together for ten to twenty seconds before moving on to the next fitting.

 Installing a New Wax Ring for Your Toilet

That ring of water around the base of the toilet can mean only one of two things; either your aim is off, or you've got a leaky wax ring on your toilet. Both have some pretty dire implications, but the leaky wax ring is the more serious of the two. Left untreated, it can quickly lead to water damage and even rot out your subfloor. And if you thought the old lady got ornery when you left the seat up, just wait until she goes crashing through the bathroom floor one night.

The good news is they're a piece of cake to replace (wax rings, not old ladies).

Toilet seals come in two basic varieties, the traditional wax ring and the newer rubber gasket style. Both types work well. Wax rings have a long track record and are basically idiot-proof, but they're messy and can melt if used in a radiant-heat floor system. The gasket style seals are slightly tougher to install, and may clog easier than wax rings, but they're clean, long lasting, and perfect for radiant heat floors.

Shut off the water to the toilet by turning off the valve under the base of the tank, then flush the toilet until the tank is empty. Use rags or a wet-dry vacuum to remove the rest of the water. Unthread the nuts holding the tank to the base, and then slide it off. You may have to unhook the water supply line, too.

Now pop off the flange bolt covers, unscrew the flange nuts, and then pull the base off the floor. Use a rag to clean off all the old wax and water, then either place the new wax ring over the flange on the floor or attach the gasket seal to the toilet base bottom. If you use a rubber seal, coat it with warm, soapy water before pushing it into the drain hole.

Be sure to tighten the flange bolts evenly when you reinstall the tank. Don't overtighten the bolts, as this can crack the porcelain. While the worst that can happen with a too-loose bowl is a little water leakage, easily fixed by a few twists of the wrench, overtighten and you can crack that expensive porcelain toilet in an instant.

 Increasing Your Showerhead Flow

"Water saver" discs, required in all new showerheads, restrict flow down to about 2.5 gallons per minute. Depending on your water pressure and the brand of showerhead you have, these water savers can make that anticipated hot morning shower feel more like a lukewarm mist. Think along the lines of the produce sprayer at the supermarket.

While nobody relishes the idea of wasting water, standing under an inadequate stream for twenty minutes is hardly practical. It's nearly impossible to purchase a showerhead without a flow restrictor, but you can easily remove or modify the flow restrictor yourself, which will produce a heavier flow.

Unscrew the showerhead assembly from the shower spout. Use a pipe wrench wrapped in a rag to remove stubborn showerheads. Most showerheads come in two pieces, so just unscrew the two pieces and look for a small rubber disc. It might be held in place by a thin, threaded nut. Remove the disc, put the showerhead back together, and hand tighten the showerhead onto the shower spout. This can make a huge difference in your morning routine.

If the flow still is uneven, or at too low pressure, try boring out the hole in the middle of the disc. Most discs have a hole an eighth of an inch, so try enlarging it to three-sixteenths or a quarter inch. Use two thin boards to sandwich the disc while boring the new hole (drill a pilot hole in one board first). This will prevent the disc from spinning. Then reinsert the disc and check water pressure and flow pattern again.

 ## Installing an Electrical Outlet/Switch

Of all the major trades, I find electrical work to be the easiest, both physically and mentally. Yet many people shy away from electrical work, refusing to even pop open the breaker box when the lights go out. While accidents still occasionally happen, modern electrical systems aren't anything to be frightened of as long as you follow some simple safety rules. Just turn off the power, make the repair, and turn the power back on. If you screwed up, the breaker will pop, and then you get to do it all over again.

I like to think of electricity as a river, with many dams, locks, and spillways along its course. The actual wire is the main channel, with the switches acting as locks and the outlets, or "plug-ins," serving as spillways where the energy is harnessed. If we can extend this comparison a little further, the breakers (or fuses, in older homes) are the dams that can cut off the flow.

First you need to locate your breaker box. This is a flat metal box, usually in your basement or utility room, and almost always on an outside wall. Open up the outside cover to reveal rows of breakers, which should be labeled on a room-by-room or appliance-by-appliance basis. If you want to work on a faulty outlet in the master bedroom, just shut off the breaker labeled Mstr. Bdrm. (or similar). Then go and check the lights *and* outlet to confirm that the power is off. Many houses will have separate breakers for the lights and outlets in one room.

If the breakers or fuses aren't labeled, plug a radio into the outlet you want to work on, pump up the volume, and flip breakers until the house goes quiet. To be really safe, use a pencil-style electrical tester to check the outlet. These light up if there's any electrical current present.

Outlets

Unscrew and remove the faceplate, then remove the two longer screws that hold the outlet in place. There are three wires running into an outlet: black, white, and copper. The black, or hot, wire always goes to the brass terminal. A common little ditty for beginner electricians is this: Black to brass to save your ass. Remember

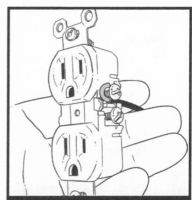

Clockwise loops close up as the screw tightens, while loops formed in the opposite direction open up and slip out.

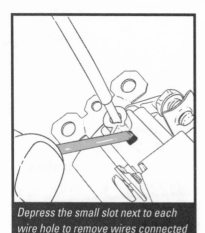

Depress the small slot next to each wire hole to remove wires connected to the back of the outlet or switch.

that and you'll be in good shape. The white, or common, wire goes to the silver screw, and the bare copper wire, or ground, goes to the green screw. If you're dealing with a faulty outlet, check the wire connections on each side first. If you need to install a new outlet, connect it the same way, making sure the loop in the wire turns clockwise.

Sometimes the wires are inserted into the holes in the back of the outlet. To remove them, depress the small slots next to the hole before pulling the wire out. These backside connections have been frowned upon by electrical inspectors and electricians I've known, probably because they're more prone to wire breaks and slip-outs.

Light Switches

If you have a standard two-way switch, there will be two black wires running to the side of the switch. The bottom wire is hot from the panel, and the top wire runs to your light. When you flip the switch you form a metal bridge and send current to the light. The common wires (white) are usually connected with a wire nut in the back of the light box. Many times light boxes double as junction boxes, so there may be a few different sets of wires inside the box. Diagnosing a faulty switch is fairly easy; disconnect the black wires, connect temporarily using a wire nut, and flip the power back on. If the light goes on, it's time to buy a new switch. If not, you have a bad connection in the wiring.

A three-way switch will have three wires: red, black, and white (plus the copper ground). Three-way switches tend to go bad a little faster than regular switches. Just make sure you install the new switch the same way as the old one, replacing one wire at a time from the old to the new switch.

73 Adjusting Sticky or Crooked Doors

Sticky, crooked, or loose-fitting doors can be irritating, and in the case of exterior doors, that cold draft can add hundreds of dollars to your heating bill. To counter this, some people resort to extra layers of weather-stripping or even shave the protruding edge off the existing door. But unless your house is located on the San Andreas Fault, your house probably hasn't shifted enough to make either approach necessary. A few minor adjustments will usually fix things right up.

If the door is dragging on the ground, your hinges may simply be worn out. Lift up on the handle; if the door moves up more than a half-inch, you've got worn-out hinges. Tap out the metal rods between the two sections of hinges, remove the door, and unscrew the old hinges. Bring them with you to the hardware store, buy new ones, and reinstall.

If the door sticks on the side, you might need to shim the corners of the door frame. But before you do this, try an old but effective trick: Make sure the hinge screws are tight, then simply wedge a magazine or checkbook in the sticky spot for a week or two. This is an easy cure for those slightly sticky doors.

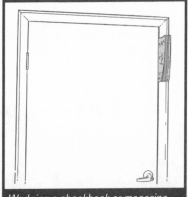

Wedging a checkbook or magazine between the door and frame for a week or two can fix those sticky spots with a minimum of hassle.

To fix those big gaps or really stuck doors, you'll need to adjust the position of the door inside the slightly larger frame, also called the rough opening. Use a flat bar and a piece of wood to remove the interior molding around the perimeter of the door, carefully prying it off so you can reuse it. Once the molding is removed you'll see wedges on each side of the door, typically three sets per side between the studs and door jamb. By adjusting the thickness of the wedges, you can move the door inside the rough opening, squaring it up for perfect fit. You may have to cut out the finishing nails that secure the doorjamb to the frame before you can adjust it.

Adjusting the door this way can be frustrating, but there's a simple trick for determining which shims to add or remove. Take a cardboard box and knock the ends out, then move the corners of the box as a model. This shows you how the door frame will move as you add or remove shims. Remember to remove shims as you add them on the other side, and vice versa. This can be a trial and error process.

Once the door is set properly, countersink a few finishing nails through the side of the doorjamb (on the non-door side of the doorstop). Then score any protruding shims with a utility knife and snap them off. Finally, set the molding back in place and nail it.

Patching Drywall

Drywall, or sheetrock, is present in almost every house. It's fireproof and easy to paint, but it also tends to develop hairline cracks as the house settles. And of course, more than a few holes have been punched, gouged, and kicked into sheetrock, leaving dents or gaping holes.

Cracks are usually fairly easy to fix. Use a caulk tube with a fine tip, fill the crack in, and paint over the whole area. If the wall is textured, you can usually imitate the pattern in small areas by dabbing diluted sheetrock mud over the repair with a paintbrush. Let the mud dry partially, then flatten it with a sheetrock knife. The results won't be perfect, but nobody will notice if you don't point it out.

To fix holes, you're going to have to make things worse before they get better. Cut out a section of drywall with a knife or rotary tool until you reach a stud on both sides of the hole, then cut the sheetrock back so half of the stud is showing on each side. A

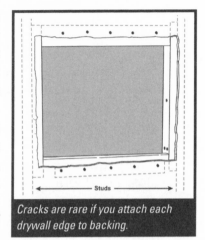

Cracks are rare if you attach each drywall edge to backing.

16" × 16" square gives you plenty of room to make your repairs and leaves you a stud to nail into on each side (studs are typically spaced 16" apart).

Toenail in two horizontal sections of two-by-four between the vertical studs, leaving half of the two-by-four revealed. Then cut out a piece of sheetrock to fit the hole and screw it into place, lightly countersinking each screw. Make sure you measure the sheetrock width before buying a replacement piece, as sheetrock comes in several different thicknesses.

Apply a thin coat of mud over the seams, then press on nonadhesive sheetrock tape with a knife (adhesive tapes are prone to cracks). Be sure to press down firmly on the tape to get rid of all the air bubbles. Fill in any screw holes, then let the mud dry for a day. Apply more mud as needed (it shrinks) allow it to dry again, and sand it smooth. Make sure you feather out the edges of the seams at least a foot or two in all directions. This will help the seams blend into the wall. Finally, prime all of the exposed mud and sheetrock and paint it to match the existing wall.

75 Shingling

Hailstorms, high winds, or ice buildup can quickly rip up asphalt shingles. The resulting water damage can occur in short order, and it's often impossible to get a roofer to your house before you suffer irreparable water damage.

Years ago, when three-tab asphalt shingles were the standard material for residential roofs, do-it-yourselfers often produced ugly roofs with crooked lines, and as a result most people just hired the job out. With the advent of architectural, or shake-style, shingles, pretty much anyone can put up, or repair, a nice-looking roof. You only need a hammer, nails, shingles, and a ladder.

Make sure you match the color and style of the old shingles when you purchase a new bundle. A bundle of shingles typically covers twenty-five to thirty-three square feet, with three to four bundles making up a "square," or a hundred square feet of finished shingle area. The average home has fifteen to twenty square of shingles.

The key to successful shingling is working from the bottom up in rows, with an alternating shingle alignment in the columns. This arrangement ensures that water flows over only finished shingle areas, and prevents seams from running more than a shingle deep.

Use a flat shovel or a heavy-tined pitchfork to remove the old or damaged shingles. Just slide the edge underneath the shingle and pry upward. You may have to go back and pull out the nails stuck in the roof boards. Cut a square of new tarpaper slightly larger than the repair area, slide it underneath the undamaged shingles, and tack it into place with a staple gun or roofing nails. Then, starting at the bottom of the exposed area, lay out a row of shingles. If you're near an eave, chimney, or valley, it may be necessary to cut the shingle with tin snips or a utility knife. If the damage involves the bottom row of shingles you'll have to double-up the shingles, using a starter strip, which is half the width of normal shingles, or you can just use a regular shingle cut in half lengthwise.

Nail above the strip of tar on the back to prevent water leakage through the nail holes. If you're laying shingles over an old layer, use slightly longer nails (usually 1¼-inch versus the standard 1-inch). If you're shingling an entire garage or house, go rent an air-powered nailer, which will save you many hours of frustration. Probably a few finger-nails, too.

The next row of shingles goes over the first row, but must be offset to prevent leakage. Again, you may need to cut the shingle to get it to fit along the edges. If you're working with architectural shingles the cut can be almost anywhere. With older, tab-style shingles, cut along one of the tabs for the best appearance. Keep repeating this until you reach the peak of the roof or the top layer of undamaged shingles. If you're tuck-ing the new shingles into the old roof, gently pry up the old shingles to get the new ones underneath. Just trim the replacement shingles to fit around the nails in the existing shingles or carefully pop out the old nails.

Don't even bother going up on your roof if it's icy, or if the roof is too steep for your comfort level. Even short falls can cause serious injury, and roofs are incredibly slippery with even a thin layer of ice. Professional roofers have special gear to traverse slick or steep roofs, and they're only a phone call away.

Make sure your shingles overlap to prevent leaks. The three-tab shingles have equal overlaps; architectural shingles can overlap basically anywhere.

149

76 Locating Studs and Using Drywall Anchors

The easiest way to locate studs is through the use of a stud finder. These handheld laser density detectors are simple to use and cost about ten bucks. Simply hold them against a section of wall that doesn't have a stud behind it, hold the button down while it calibrates, then slide it horizontally until it beeps. That's your stud. If your readings aren't spaced sixteen or twenty-four inches apart, you probably calibrated on a stud. Pick a new section and try again.

If you don't have a stud finder, try tapping lightly on the wall with a hammer or your fist. Spaces between studs will sound hollow, while the areas behind them will give a solid-sounding thud. This method is far from foolproof, and is even tougher when working with an insulated wall. A better method involves measuring from an established stud location, such as a solidly anchored nail, or a room corner. The next stud should be either sixteen or twenty-four inches away from that stud location, and so on down the length of the wall.

Of course, it's one of the immutable laws of nature that the perfect spot to hang a picture or shelf will have nothing but dead space behind the sheetrock. Instead of moving your wall hanging to a less-than-perfect spot, simply install a drywall anchor at the desired location. You can then twist a screw right into the anchor to provide a sturdy, picture-perfect location.

Drywall anchors come in quite a few different styles, but generally the larger, more complex anchors will hold more weight. The anchor package will show the diameter you need to drill in the sheetrock. Once the hole is drilled, simply push the anchor in flush with the finished wall surface, and then twist in a screw. Make sure you drill the hole exactly the right diameter; too big and the anchor will slide through and drop into the wall space, too small and the sheetrock will crack when you try to push it flush.

The screw will cause the sides of the drywall anchor to expand, and the resulting screw base can be strong enough to hold pictures, shelving, or even flat-screen televisions. Of course, check the load rating on the anchors before trusting a 25-cent anchor with a $2,000 television.

 ## Sharpening a Knife

A good, sharp knife is one of the most useful things you can carry in your pocket, but a dull knife is about as useless as tits on a bull. And, strange as it may sound, the most dangerous knives are also the ones with dull blades. That's because people tend to apply excessive force trying to cut through something with a dull blade, causing the knife to slip.

Most knives made in the past twenty years have stainless steel blades, which don't rust and are harder than regular steel. Unfortunately, they're also a little harder to put an edge on. If you're working with stainless steel, plan on spending about twice as long sharpening as you would with conventional steel. On the plus side, stainless steel blades hold their edge longer than regular steel.

All knife blades are actually saws, with microscopic teeth. When these teeth become dull or bent, the knife will quickly lose its efficiency. The easiest way to keep an edge on a knife is by using a steel (a thin metal file with a wood or plastic handle). Press the blade against the steel just above the handle, at about a twenty-degree angle, then pull the knife up and out while maintaining constant pressure. Repeat a few times, then move on to the other side. This will quickly straighten and sharpen the teeth on the blade edge. If you're butchering or whittling, a few strokes on the steel every fifteen to twenty minutes will keep your knife sharp

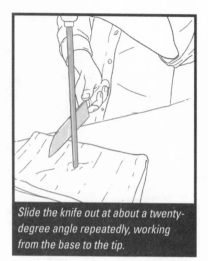

Slide the knife out at about a twenty-degree angle repeatedly, working from the base to the tip.

throughout the process. The steel straightens those microscopic teeth, narrowing down the cutting edge to a fine, perfectly aligned row.

After a while, however, those microscopic teeth wear down and disappear. When this happens, you need to use a whetstone to regrind the edge of the blade and create more cutting teeth. Most whetstones will have different grit sizes on both flat edges and one edge. Wet the stone (mineral oil is fine, but so is plain old spit) and slide the blade over the stone in a circular motion, starting with the coarsest side and moving to the finer-grained side. Wet the stone frequently; a dry stone is basically useless, because the steel dust plugs the sandpaper-like qualities of the stone.

Check the knife's sharpness by pressing the edge lightly against the back of your thumbnail at about a forty-five degree angle. If it slides off, the blade is still dull. If it bites into the nail, it's sharp enough to work with. If you can shave hair off the back of your hand you've achieved a fine razor edge, which is nice for a little while, but it will quickly wear down into a regular old sharp blade. Use the whetstone once or twice a year, saving the steel for daily or weekly sharpenings.

78 Changing and Sharpening Lawnmower Blades

The day I bought my first riding lawnmower was a pretty proud day. It was big and shiny and had a beer holder built right into the fender, one of the major selling points. Of course, I simply couldn't wait to try it out. My wife and I had recently built a house, and had excavated lots of earth to build a basement, so our lawn resembled a minefield more than a true lawn, but I didn't let that deter me. I figured I could weave in and out of the patches of grass—hell, I figured this thing could have done the moguls at the local dirt track if I wanted it to.

I think I made it about 100 feet before I heard a tremendous crash and a boulder shot out through–not under but *through*—the deck. I shut the mower off, and with the expression of a guy about to look at some X-rays he really doesn't want to see, peered underneath the deck.

You know, sometimes the new doesn't wear off something. No, sometimes the new just *falls* off it.

Well, I'm hardly alone. I'd wager at least half of all riding and push mowers have nicked, dull, or damaged blades. Badly damaged blades can cause the shaft to warp, which can actually ruin your mower's engine. Dull blades, while they won't damage the mower, tend to crush instead of cut, damaging the grass and resulting in an unhealthy lawn.

Unless the blade is badly damaged, you can usually remove it and sharpen the blade yourself. A flat file or grinding wheel both work, but I've found a power sander puts an excellent edge on heavy blades with a minimum of effort (it also works great for sharpening axes and hatchets).

Simply tip push mowers up to get at the blades with the air filter up to prevent oil from draining into the cylinder. While it's possible to work on a riding mower by simply raising the deck, you may want to jack it up and block it, or drive the front end up on some car ramps.

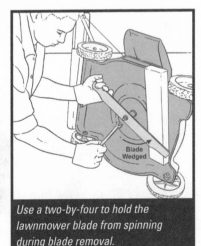

Blade
Wedged

Use a two-by-four to hold the lawnmower blade from spinning during blade removal.

The blades are held in place by a nut on the bottom of the shaft, but you can't simply loosen it up, as the blade will rotate with the nut. While you can sometimes slip another wrench onto the shaft above the blade, it's easier to wedge a two-by-four board under the deck, then turn the nut until the mower blade bites into the wood. If you have tandem blades, mark the bottom of each blade so you put them back in the right way. If you're buying new blades, bring the old ones to the store to ensure you get a matching set.

Drilling

There are two keys to successful drilling: Use quality bits, and operate at the right speed. This is especially important with hard materials, such as steel or concrete. A quality drill bit set will not only make drilling much easier, but it will also last a lot longer than economy-type bits. I've had cheap bits literally disintegrate when they touched metal—they weren't worth the plastic case they came in.

Given the right bit and drill speed, it's easy to punch holes through just about any material with a minimum of effort. Wood is the most common material for the average handyman, and it's also one of the easiest to work with. Wood bits, or paddle bits, have a flared end with a sharp point, with the size of the bit stamped right into the metal. On each side of the point is a blade that is designed to cut through wood. You can always tell how sharp your paddle bit is by the size of the shavings; big shavings mean a sharp bit, while a bit that produces dust is boring, rather than cutting, through the wood. If you're working on material where appearance is important, make sure you drill from the finished side in. Wood bits often create an outward explosion of splinters and chips when they exit the board.

For holes larger than an inch in diameter, use a hole saw. These bits, which are cylinders with saw teeth on the bottom, screw directly into your drill and have a regular drill bit located in the middle. Use the slots on the side to pry material out of the interior once you've drilled through the board.

Drilling through steel is slightly trickier. Again, quality bits are extremely important; the best of them have diamond tips and are made out of hardened steel. The most common mistake when working with steel is drilling too fast. Cut at the lowest speed setting, working up only slowly, adding a couple of drops of honing or cutting oil to reduce heat. You can always tell if you're cutting at the right speed by watching the steel waste coming off the bit. A sharp bit, operated at the right speed, will curl steel off the bit in long, winding strings. When drilling stainless or tempered steel, both of which are harder than conventional steel, you'll need to drill pilot holes first, then work up to the final size bit.

Drilling through concrete requires a special masonry bit. These bits have a thick, short, triangular blade at the end of the bit, and are best used with drills that have a hammer function. These types of drills work like a sort of jackhammer, crushing the cement instead of cutting through it. A masonry bit used in conjunction with a hammer drill can quickly cut holes in cement, brick, or stone.

80 Operating a Circular Saw

When working with circular saws, it's essential to have a sharp blade. Dull blades create bad cuts and are dangerous to boot, since they can produce kickbacks (if you haven't experienced this, imagine the saw reversing direction in a split second). If your saw smokes or hesitates when cutting through a board, it's time to switch out the blades. They're safer, and you'll get a better cut, too.

While circular saws are designed to make long, straight cuts, attempting even a subtle shift in direction can cause the saw to bind. The easiest

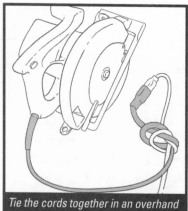

Tie the cords together in an overhand knot first, leaving about six inches of loose end, then connect.

way to get around this is to cut faster. Like a guy who runs across a tightrope, it's a lot easier to stay on course the faster you go. Setting your blade depth just deep enough to make the cut will also help prevent binding. There's a setting on the side of the saw that adjusts the fence depth, which in turn regulates blade depth.

Another common problem occurs when making long cuts on a sheet of plywood or chipboard. As you cut, the hanging portion of the sheet will sag, causing the saw to bind. While you can sometimes hold the sagging section up with your free hand or a sawhorse, it's usually easier to just set the sheets on runners, with each side of the cut balanced and supported. Set the blade just deep enough to cut through the board, and if necessary run it right over the runners.

Another trivial but irritating problem occurs when the saw becomes unplugged halfway through your cut. Many times simple tension makes them come unplugged, other times the plug end gets caught on the sawhorse or the far end of the cut in the board. To keep the saw running, tie the extension cord and the saw cord together using a regular overhand knot, and then plug them together. It's almost impossible to pull the cords apart when they're tied like this, and I rarely plug in any power tool, saw or otherwise, without taking a few seconds to ensure continuous power.

Split-free Screwing

Screws work great to bind two materials together, and they have the added bonus of being a lot easier to remove than nails if you make a mistake. The downside is they're much slower to install than nails, and they have a tendency to split wood, causing unseemly cracks. Those cracks also lessen holding power.

All you have to do to avoid splits is drill a pilot hole first, which is simply a hole slightly smaller than the diameter of the screw. Clamp the pieces together first, drill your pilot holes, and sink the screws in. You might want to put a couple of screws in right away to increase holding power while you drill the remainder of the pilot holes. This is the old tried-and-true method, and it works just about every time. But it's slow, especially when you have to keep changing bits between the pilot and driver bits.

Another, faster technique is to clamp the edges of the wood before screwing. This method reduces the outward pressure on the wood grain, and since wood will always split along the grain, you get a quick, one-bit solution to the cracking problem.

SECTION 5

Social

General Disclaimer: If you're an average guy, you've probably witnessed or participated in some inherently dangerous activity. For some reason, we get away with a lot of stuff that flies in the face of physics, the advertised effectiveness of local law enforcement, and the hypothesis of a stern, non-fun-loving deity.

While relatively tame in comparison to some of the things we've all been a part of—or probably will be—the inclusion of the following various how-to information does not imply that using the information is necessarily a good idea, especially in combination. Believe me, the simultaneous use of beer bongs and potato guns can be deadly.

And speaking of beer bongs and shotgunning beer and downing shots . . . well, just take it easy. Your body can handle a drink an hour. Much more than that, and odds are your liver isn't the only thing that's going to end up being disgusted with you at the end of the night.

Tapping a Keg

It seems like nearly every big social event with friends and family involves a keg or two of beer. Handled, tapped, and set properly, keg beer supplies a steady stream of cold brew that bites into the back of your throat just like canned or bottled beer. Too many times, though, kegs produce piles of foam on top of tiny amounts of liquid. Or, when a carbon dioxide (CO_2) system is used, the beer comes out supersaturated with carbon dioxide. I still remember the absolutely excruciating headache that sidelined a couple of my best friends and me the night of my bachelor party, all because the gas setting on the keg CO_2 regulator was too high. At the end of the night we had so much carbon dioxide in our system that plants would burst into full bloom when we walked past.

A keg of beer is basically just an overgrown soda pop can. Shake it, and it's going to foam and spray. It stands to reason, then, that the single most important thing in producing quality tap beer is to keep it as cold and motionless as possible. This means the keg should be picked up and iced at least twenty-four hours before the big party. It takes a long time for the contents to settle down once they get shaken up, and foamy or flat beer has tainted many a backyard event.

You can never have too much ice on a keg of beer. Just set the keg in a barrel with a slightly wider diameter, and line the bottom with ice. Pack the sides and top with more ice, then cover with an old blanket. Drill a small hole in the bottom of the barrel to let the meltwater out. It's literally impossible to get a keg of beer to freeze by adding ice, but easy to underestimate how much ice it takes to keep a big jug of beer cold on a hot summer day.

Once everything is iced and settled down, it's time to tap the keg. If you're using a ball tapper, simply line up the slots, push it down, and twist it. You might get a little spray on you, but that's okay—it drives the ladies crazy. You'll have to pump the keg as the interior pressure diminishes, but try not to add too much pressure right away. No matter how careful you are, the first few glasses of beer are going to be a little foamy. Just pour the first stream of beer into a pitcher and let it settle.

Carbon dioxide keg systems are the professional choice of bars and basement home brewers across the country. These systems have a refrigerator to keep everything cool, and a gas cylinder that injects CO_2 right into the keg, eliminating the manual pumping required with a ball tapper. The problem most people run into when using this system is determining the right pressure on the regulator. The correct setting is 10–12 PSI for lower elevations, slightly less than that at higher elevations. Low pressure equals flat beer, while a high setting produces frothy beer—or, occasionally, normal-looking beer that produces one of those splitting headaches.

Since a keg has internal pressure to begin with, set it about 3 PSI lower when you first tap it. Then adjust the pressure upward as the internal gases are depleted. If you have long supply lines running from the tapper to the keg, add a little more pressure. For a foolproof method with clear lines, just start low and adjust the pressure upward slowly until the bubbles in the line disappear.

 ## 83 Shotgunning a Beer

Nothing says "enjoy in moderation" like jamming a knife into the bottom of a beer can, popping the top, and pouring the entire contents down your throat in five seconds flat. But you've got to try shotgunning a beer at least once, and it's nice to do it without making an ass of yourself.

The problem most people run into when shotgunning a beer is trying to swallow it like they would a regular drink. This won't work; you'll just end up spitting the beer out and foaming at the mouth like a rabid dog, and that's an inexcusable waste of beer.

While conventional shotgunning dictates that you need to "open up" your throat, this is a physical impossibility. Instead, you need to minimize the swallowing action. Once you've got this down, the rest of the mechanics of shotgunning a beer are pretty simple.

You'll need a can of beer, unopened and at least cool, preferably not ice-cold but certainly not warm. Then, using a knife, ice pick, pen, or other pointy object, punch a hole in the bottom of the can, and immediately cover it with your thumb. If you use a knife, give it a little twist to open up the hole. Then quickly pop the tab and tilt the can back as if taking a normal drink. With airflow unimpeded, the beer will flow straight out, without the typical gurgling, stop-and-go stream. Drinking from the regular drinking part of the can ensures that you won't cut your mouth on the jagged edges of the hole that you've created, although some people choose to shotgun beer that way.

To minimize the swallowing action, press your tongue down and "flex" the back of your throat. Done right, you'll immediately feel the throat area expand. It's close to a gagging action. Pour the beer back and relax your throat slightly; the beer should slide right down your gullet and straight to your stomach (and then, probably, to your over-taxed liver).

Sometimes you can't quite get it all down. If you're dealing with rela-tively inexperienced onlookers, crumpling the not-quite-empty can and throwing it to the ground victoriously will usually accomplish your goal (assuming looking cool is the goal, not dehydration).

 ## Making and Using a Beer Bong

The softball tournaments my old team attended were mostly about par-tying, with winning—hell, just showing up at the ballfield—coming in a distant second. One tournament in particular comes to mind. We played a total of one game the first day, with the opposing team neglect-ing to show up. This schedule, I've come to believe, was designed by the local bar.

Many hours later we headed back to the campsite, consumed by that inexplicable twenty-something desire to drink ourselves into an even more obnoxious state. Some idiot (me) had booked us into a state campground where alcohol was prohibited, which we cheerfully ignored. Since slamming a beer wasn't fast enough, we used a funnel with a long tube to pump even more beer into our systems. This elegant contraption, commonly called a beer bong, has a brain cell kill count well into the godzillions. (By the way—if a cop ever asks, these fun-nels are for adding antifreeze to your truck, which has a cracked block. There is at least one park-roaming law officer in central Minnesota who will believe you.)

There is absolutely nothing on this planet that will make beer enter your body faster than a beer bong. Unlike its illegal counterpart, a beer bong does not purify or otherwise enhance beer. It just makes it go down faster, and in this case it nearly got us expelled from the campsite and made all our hair fall out. No, come to think of it, the hair loss was from the haircuts we gave each other at three in the morning. Either way, the end result wasn't pretty.

The beauty of this particular beer bong was the stopcock, which paused the beer until we could position the funnel into our mouths. While it's relatively easy to fit a piece of tubing onto a funnel end (the funnel should hold at least twelve ounces), restraining the flow until you're ready is the important part. It adds drama. If you use tubing that's soft and flexible, you can simply kink the tube or use a small clamp to pinch it shut. Commercial funnels with built-in stopcocks are the best, but beware those stopcocks with reduced flow-through capabilities. After all, a bonged beer ain't no sipping drink.

Just open it up, then swallow like you would a shotgunned beer.

Downing a Shot Without Making a Face

Here's the thing: Almost any shot of cheap booze, poured straight off the shelf, is going to cause your body to react in a "get-it-out" manner. The particular reaction varies from person to person, from a mild pinching of the eyes and puckering to actual gagging and spit-ups. But unless it's a smooth drink and you're a couple sheets to the wind, there's going to be an inherent reaction that can diminish your otherwise tough appearance.

Yet no matter how strong the shot—and yes, I'm talking to you, Lord Calvert—it's usually not the taste that gets you. High-proof liquor exists in both liquid and gaseous states, and the fumes caused by tossing a shot back often fill your mouth and nose with alcohol gases. This is an unnatural and undesirable feeling; the common reaction is to shut your eyes and pinch your mouth, then breath out from the back of your throat. This further volates the alcohol, which triggers the gag reflex and makes you look like a pansy.

Do *not* take a deep breath before downing a shot. Once the shot is downed a quick exhale will only give you a second shot of vapors. This aftereffect is the real enemy when it comes to keeping a straight face and is exacerbated by lusty exhales and nose breathing. Avoid these, and you're halfway there. Exhale, then toss the drink back, getting it past your tongue as quickly as possible. Swallow immediately.

Now all you have to worry about is the fumes. Don't breath in immediately, but simply open your mouth slightly. After a few seconds, breathe in shallowly through your mouth (not your nose!). This will keep volatization to a minimum.

The only real foolproof way to down a shot of whiskey without flinching is to squirt a shot of lemon juice into your mouth immediately before the shot. The resulting pucker closes everything off in your mouth, and the shot goes down as smooth as melted butter. Careful, though—what goes down also comes up, and the return trip isn't always as smooth.

86 Smoking a Cigar

I remember well the anticipation before smoking my first Cuban cigar. It had been smuggled in from Mexico, and there were four or five of us waiting longingly to enjoy a fine smoking experience on a warm spring day. The general consensus? The twelve-dollar cigar tasted like shit.

The reasons for this are many, and none of them have to do with the initial quality of the cigar. Cigars are meant to be smoked within a few days of being removed from the humidor, and this one had been out a week or more. Probably being packed in a suitcase of sweaty socks and underwear didn't help, either. Additionally, we had smoked a strong cigar, which tasted bitter to our unconditioned palates. At that time I smoked a pack of cigarettes a day, but even I couldn't stand the taste. Out of habit, I inhaled the cigar smoke—another big no-no. After a couple drags, I felt like a kid sucking on cornshuck cigarettes behind the barn.

If you want to enjoy a cigar, purchase it right before you smoke it. This ensures the tobacco is moist and flavorful. Choose a mild cigar for the best taste; much like any connoisseur, you'll acquire stronger tastes only after you become acclimated to the basic flavors. A good drink such as scotch, brandy, or a Kahlua-based coffee drink helps complement the flavor of the cigar.

Cut the cigar through the head, which is nearest to the label, immediately before you smoke it. While you might see screen actors bite the end off a cigar, this usually rips the wrapping and causes the cigar to unravel. Use a sharp single- or double-blade guillotine cigar cutter to snip the head right before it reaches the thickest, main section of the stogie.

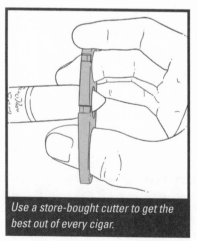

Use a store-bought cutter to get the best out of every cigar.

Lacking a cigar cutter, use scissors or a sharp knife. Some people even use a pencil to enlarge the small hole in the end, but this method reduces smoke flow and might require a lot more suction than any guy should really display in the company of other men. In fact, some folks cut the cigar at a forty-five-degree angle to increase the amount of smoke. If you use a regular knife, cut completely around the cigar and then pull the end off. Dull blades and slow cuts compress the end of the cigar, resulting in reduced smoke flow. If your cutter is dull, just leave the cellophane wrapper on for a cleaner cut.

Light the cigar with a match or butane lighter, sucking from the cut end and rotating the cigar as you apply the flame. Repeat this rotation as you smoke. Since the cigar is tobacco from end to end, you can smoke it right down to the nub, but it often starts to taste ashy when you get down to the last couple of inches.

87 Shuffling and Dealing Cards Like a Pro

A sloppy deal during a game of cards is bound to piss some people off, whether it's a penny-ante game of poker or a $20-per-hand game of blackjack. Inadvertently flashing the bottom of the deck while dealing, spilling the cards all over the floor during the shuffle, or ignoring basic dealing etiquette isn't cool, and the people you're playing against aren't going to be very impressed. Done right, a thorough shuffle and level deal evens the playing field; done incorrectly and it's like the clerk scratching off your lottery ticket after you buy it.

The best way to evenly distribute the cards is to combine two or more techniques, usually a fine and a coarse shuffle. A coarse shuffle quickly separates groups of cards, while a fine shuffle separates individual cards. Most casinos have to shuffle at least seven times to ensure randomness, but that's a lot of shuffling for private poker parties. A couple of overhand shuffles followed by two or three riffle shuffles produces a good, fast mix. If you're playing with a new deck, feel free to spread the cards out across the table and mix them up before the actual shuffle.

The overhand shuffle is a perfect coarse shuffle. Use your right hand to pick up the deck lengthwise, with your thumb on one end of the deck and your middle and ring fingers on the other end. Hold your left

Overhand Shuffle: *Just let a portion of the cards slide out, move the deck forward, and repeat.*

Riffle Shuffle: *The correct finger pressures for the riffle shuffle can only be learned by lots of practice (solitaire being the preferred game for practicing).*

hand underneath the deck, slightly cupped. Relax your fingertips enough to let a few cards slip through your grip and into your left hand, where they'll rest against your fingers. Then move the deck forward and let more cards fall in front of those cards, until the entire deck is in your left hand. Repeat the whole process a couple more times, then move onto the fine shuffle.

A riffle shuffle has two main things going for it: It effectively and quickly randomizes the cards, and it also looks like you know what you're doing. An inexperienced shuffler usually means an inexperienced card player, a cue that crafty card sharks quickly pick up on. A riffle shuffle is relatively easy to master, but you'll want to practice for a little while before the big poker party.

Grab a deck and square it up by tapping it on the table. Turn the deck lengthwise, with your middle and ring fingers holding the sides. Bend your index finger so the last knuckle is pressed against the middle of the deck, forcing the middle of the deck to bulge outward. Relax the pressure on your thumb, which will let the cards snap down onto the table. The sound should resemble muted machine gun fire.

Stop when half the cards have hit the table, then pick them up with your left hand. Tap the edges to even that half, then arrange the two sections so they're facing each other at a slight angle. Use the same technique you used to separate the deck to let the cards flow into each other. Once the cards are gone, you can simply push them together using your palms, or better yet, bend them up into an arch, with your thumbs forming an overhead bridge.

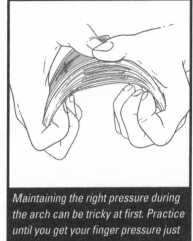

Maintaining the right pressure during the arch can be tricky at first. Practice until you get your finger pressure just right.

Slide the cards together enough so about the top third are in contact with the other half, then push down on the base of the cards with your palm and in on the sides. This is where the practice comes in; experiment with hand and fingertip pressure until the cards bend into an arch, then slide back together.

Once you're done dealing, offer the person to your right (who passed you the deal) the option to cut by sliding the shuffled deck over to him. If he doesn't want to cut (many people don't, but it's nice to ask) he'll just tap the top of the deck. If he slides off a section of the deck and places it on the table, place the other half on top of this cut section and deal. Do not shuffle again after somebody has cut the deck.

88 Throwing a Good Poker Party

The most important ingredient of a good poker game is having compatible players. It doesn't matter if your friends are serious card aficionados, or if their card-playing skills are based solely on years of slapjack practice—you can have a good time playing with either group. The key is to avoid mixing the two, especially if you have one very good player matched up with a bunch of amateurs, or a table of card sharks and some grunt with wads of cash and a full complement of tells. Hard feelings are bound to occur in either of these scenarios, and that's not what poker parties are about.

After you get the right bunch of guys together, get rid of the cash money. It's always easier to pay for something with a check or credit card instead of cash, and poker chips work in the same manner. Have everyone buy in for a set amount, then distribute chips. Substituting chips for cash means faster games, bigger pots, and a more relaxed atmosphere. Even professional poker players on cable television would be hard-pressed to bluff effectively with $1 million in actual greenbacks sitting in front of him.

Once these two essential tasks are complete, all that remains are the creature comforts. Poker tables are nice but by no means essential; comfortable chairs are also a welcome bonus. Poker parties are often a great excuse to smoke and cuss, so for domesticated men the drafty old garage or basement might be a better fit than the kitchen table. The key is to form a relaxed environment that is free of inhibitions, which translates into bigger bets and faster games (it's a lot more fun, too). Drinks work in the same capacity, of course, but also consider having a pot of coffee ready for the end of the night.

If playing more than one type of game, make sure everyone knows how to play the type of game before you deal (the dealer will call the game, unless you're playing a winner-take-all game like Texas hold 'em).

Many times the dealer will be the only one to ante, with people having to call the ante to stay in the game. This is called a pot game (it's different than the one you played in college). Otherwise, you can always play standard poker, with everyone putting in an ante. The advantage of a dealer-only ante, or a pot game, is that a string of bad cards won't nickel-and-dime you to death. You only have to get in when you deal, or when you think you have a great hand.

89 Playing Blackjack

It was a Friday night in Vegas, and seven of us wandered into a casino well-oiled and primed to donate cash. Within a half hour only a couple of us remained, the other guys having either lost all their money or been thrown out by security guards after violating house rules. My remaining friend and I were doing better, but only because we were following the most basic of blackjack rules. Yup—we flirted with the overweight dealer, and she in turn waved the guards off when we broke card protocol.

Actually, we also obeyed the most commonsense rules in playing blackjack. We didn't hit when the dealer had anything between a six and two showing (unless we had a total of under eleven in our hand), we split aces and eights, and we didn't bend our cards up or touch our money once we pushed it in for a bet.

No matter how much fun you're having, you should never lose money fast at blackjack. Blackjack and craps are two games in which the house does not have a definitive edge, and you're much better off playing blackjack than plunking quarters into a slot machine—provided you know what you're doing.

Many folks like to try to pick a "hot" table, which of course is basically nonsense. It's much better to find a table where you can position yourself at third base, which is immediately to the right of the dealer. This means you'll be the last player to get a card, so you'll see the most cards before you decide whether to hit.

Once you're in position, cash in for some chips. Don't get a bunch of chips; dragging out your wallet every half hour or so can have a sobering effect. Push your bet into the designated circle, and then don't touch it until the dealer takes it or adds to it.

All you need to do to win is get a higher hand than the dealer without going over twenty-one. If you go over twenty-one, you lose automatically, even if the dealer goes over later. Face cards are worth ten, and the rest of the cards are worth their face value. The one exception is the ace, which can be either one or eleven. It's your choice, and the ace value is arbitrary, automatically shifting from one to eleven to give you the best hand as you take additional cards, or hits.

Both of your cards go face down. The dealer's cards will be split; one down, one showing. Do not bend your cards to look at them; pick them up and then set them back down. In nearly every casino, it's assumed that a guy who bends his cards is trying to mark them, and they'll boot you on general principles. If you're lucky, you'll end up with an embarrassing warning first.

The dealer's face-up card dictates how you'll play each game. Face cards, which are worth ten points, make up the greatest collective portion of any deck (tens are worth ten points, too). The suit doesn't matter. To play blackjack effectively, you have to assume the dealer's face-down card is worth ten points. If the dealer is showing a two, three, four, five, or six (bust cards) assume he has a twelve through a sixteen hand. The dealer *must* hit on anything totaling sixteen or less, and must stay on seventeen. Never take a card when the dealer is showing a bust card, unless you have cards totaling eleven or less and can't possibly go over. Following that simple rule will make you welcome at any blackjack table, and will also increase your winnings.

If the dealer is showing an ace, he'll offer insurance, and you can bet half your original bet. If the dealer's down card then turns out to be a face card, you win two to one. Any card other than a face card and you lose it all. Avoid insurance—it's a sucker bet.

To indicate you want a hit, tap the table with a finger or your cards, or say, "Hit me." When you want to stay, turn your cards horizontally. The dealer may still ask you if you want another hit; just shake your head or say no.

Splitting cards is a good idea on a pair of eights or aces; neither pair makes a great hand in itself, but is worth eighteen or twenty-one, respectively, when split and paired with a face card. You only get one hit per card when you split. Just spread the cards apart and put your original bet under one card, and the same amount under the other card. A total of twenty-one on a split does not pay out three to two, like a regular blackjack does. Splitting makes the most sense when the dealer has a bust card.

 Playing Craps

Craps isn't nearly as difficult as it looks, and it has one of the best odds of winning in the casino. It's also a helluva lot of fun, probably because it's the only game where you win, or lose, right along with all the other players.

Look closely at the craps table picture and you'll see that the table is divided into two halves. This is only done to increase playing space. The only thing you need to understand about the table for basic craps play is the location of the pass line; this is where you place your bet.

Craps is about betting on the dice thrower to hit a certain number, and avoid others. Everybody at the table not employed by the casino is on the same side, creating a feeling of camaraderie and teamwork. Two dice are rolled, so the possible numbers range from two to twelve. Betting is easy; put your chips on the pass line and hope the shooter does well.

How You Win

1. The shooter rolls seven or eleven on his come-out roll. A come-out roll is simply the first roll after money is won or lost; one shooter may have several consecutive come-out rolls.

2. The shooter rolls a point number (four, five, six, eight, nine, or ten), then matches it on a following roll. So, if you get a six on the first roll, then roll six again, you win (and so does everyone who bet with you). The dealer will put a white "buck" on the point number after the come-out roll.

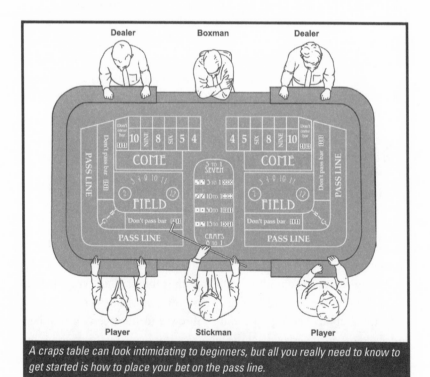

A craps table can look intimidating to beginners, but all you really need to know to get started is how to place your bet on the pass line.

How You Lose

1. The shooter rolls a two, three, or twelve on his come-out roll.
2. The shooter rolls a seven or eleven after *his* come-out roll. This is the most confusing part to first-time craps players. Just remember that seven and eleven are good at first, and then you don't want to see them until a new come-out roll.

Easy enough. Note that the two, three, and twelve mean nothing after the come-out roll. Shooting numbers besides seven, eleven, or the point number also means nothing—except another roll for the shooter. The shooter keeps rolling the dice until he "seven-outs," or rolls a seven while trying to match a point number.

There are more ways to win and lose with other types of bets, but that's the easiest way to start out. You bet by simply placing chips on the pass line area directly in front of you. Usually you need to bet at the start of a series, before someone's come-out roll. You'll know because the buck will be black and to the side (it says OFF). If the buck is on a point, betting is off until the series is over. Some dealers will allow you to place a bet anytime before a throw, but most casinos traditionally allow bets only at the beginning of each series. Just ask the dealer if you're unsure.

Get chips at the table by placing your money on the table, in front of the dealer. Don't hand it to him; set it on the table. Make sure nobody's rolling the dice when you put your money down—the crowd'll be downright ornery if you messed up a hot shooter's streak. Start out with low bets until you get the hang of it; ask the dealer for nickels ($5 chips).

The stick man passes the dice clockwise. When it's your turn, the stick man will pass you four to six dice. Choose only two, and shake them *with one hand*—use both hands and they'll think you're trying

175

to palm loaded dice into the game. The dice need to hit the far wall on one end and bounce back for the roll to be valid. Keep rolling until you seven-out. Even rolling consecutive automatic losses on your come-out roll doesn't mean you get to pass the dice—though you might wish it did. Just remember, you don't have to bet each throw, even if you're the one throwing the dice.

Placing a Sports Bet

I placed my first real football bets in 1998, when the Minnesota Vikings started out their season 7–0 and finished up 15–1. Four-time Super Bowl losers and known chokers, it took the betting community a little while to get behind the Vikes. Yet the Vikings kept winning by more than the expected amount (the point spread, or line) and I was one happy dude. I won several hundred dollars that year, most of which left my pockets after a disastrous NFC Championship showing. Big surprise.

While I thought I had the betting scene figured out back in '98, it hasn't been nearly as easy since. Nonetheless, nothing adds a little excitement to an otherwise boring game than having the week's grocery money riding on that final, pointless field goal.

The most basic bet is a simple line bet on one team. If, for example, the Bears are playing the Seahawks, and the Bears are favored by seven, then you have two options. If you bet on the Bears, they have to win by more than seven points (a tie, called a push, goes to the house). Bet on the Seahawks (to sound savvy you'd say, "I'll take the Seahawks and the points") and you collect if they win, or even if they lose by six points or less. If you make a straight bet on this type of game, betting and winning on the Seahawks would give you more than even money (if you bet $20 and win, you might get $25 back). Bet and win on the Bears straight-up and you'd net maybe $15.

Anytime you lose, you lose not just your original bet but also an additional portion of that bet, called the juice. So, betting $100 and losing might mean you pay $110 or $120. Unlike you, oddsmakers aren't in this for fun.

Another common type of bet is called an over-under bet, which is the expected composite score total. If the Bears-Seahawks game's over-under is forty-six, and you think the defenses are going to have a big day, you'd take the under. It doesn't matter if the Bears score forty-two and the Seahawks score three; the total (forty-five in this case) is what matters, not the respective contributions.

Combining one or more bets is called a parlay and will pay better odds depending on how many bets make up the parlay. You can take the Bears over the Seahawks, take the under in the Chargers-Rams game, and then take the Vikes and the points in their underdog match against the St. Catherine Holy Terrors. Winning all three means you could win six to one against your original bet ($20 gets you $120). Losing any one of the three (again, a push is a loss) means you lose the entire bet. The juice may be a little higher, too. Bottom line: Parlays, fun as they are, are a bit of a sucker bet. You can also use teasers, which allow you to move the line up or down a certain amount. The payouts for teaser parlays are lower than for straight parlays.

Betting futures is a long-term investment. For this type of bet you typically choose a team to win the championship at the beginning of the season, at the posted odds. Betting on the Yankees to win the World Series might give you five bucks for every dollar bet. If you put twenty on the Vikes to win the Superbowl and it happens, you can go tell Trump *he's* fired.

It's easy enough to find a sports book, either by phone, over the Internet, or in person. Tell them the bet you want, and then work out payment procedures beforehand. Size doesn't really matter, but smaller books typically have lower juice, while major Vegas or overseas outlets will have some unusual bets, such as cumulative number of first downs, receiving yards per player, and so on. They'll also have higher juice. Rules vary on a state-by-state basis for placing and accepting bets, so check first if you're worried about breaking a pointless law.

 Building a Potato Gun

These things are wicked, and aiming one at a person is not much different than pointing a real gun at somebody. I remember vividly when a friend smashed a dent in someone's metal tailgate with a well-placed tater. Spud guns are great, if slightly juvenile, fun, but they move fast and they hit hard. Be careful, and never point it at a person or animal.

For a few bucks you can purchase all the materials and a sack of spuds, and in return you get a weapon that can launch edible food at over 200 feet per second. This is some fine, not to mention cheap, entertainment. There are three basic parts to any functional spud gun: the barrel, the combustion chamber, and the igniter. These can be modified slightly, so feel free to experiment. Once you have everything, simply glue them together with PVC cement.

Spud Gun Parts List
1. A 24"–48" length of 1½" or 2" PVC pipe (barrel)
2. A 12"–24" length of 3" or 4" PVC (combustion chamber)
3. A reducer coupling to connect the barrel and combustion chamber
4. A threaded end cap and female bushing for the end of the combustion chamber
5. A couple of screws (optional) and a BBQ lighter or a twist-style lantern igniter
6. Spuds
7. Aerosol hairspray or a propane torch

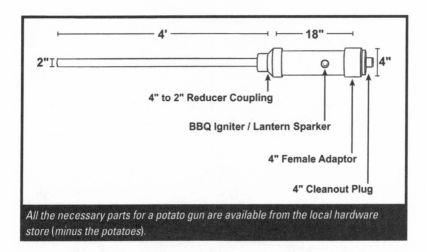

All the necessary parts for a potato gun are available from the local hardware store (minus the potatoes).

Use primer and PVC glue to connect all the fittings, and make sure you do a good job, since leaks will lessen the power of launch, and can cause flames to spurt out the side of the combustion chamber.

File down the muzzle so it's sharp, which will help cut the spud down to a perfect size when you load it up. Attach the igniter wire on the BBQ lighter to the screws so that a spark crosses when you pull the trigger. If there isn't a spark, move the screws closer together. As an alternative, you can also drill a hole in the side of the combustion chamber and insert a twist-style lantern igniter. Be sure to silicone around the edges.

Load the spud from the muzzle, forcing it down the barrel to a point just above the combustion chamber. Use a stick or pipe to push it down to the base of the barrel. It should be a tight fit, since loose spuds don't go very far. This is where the filed edges of the barrel can be used to cut bigger potatoes down to the perfect size.

Once the spud is loaded, unscrew the end cap and give the combustion chamber a shot of propane or aerosol hairspray. You'll need to experiment a little to get the right air/gas mixture; start out on the low side and work your way up. Quickly screw the end cap back on to seal the gases, aim the gun somewhere safe, and hit the igniter. Not exactly opera-night entertainment, but plain old fun nonetheless.

Opening a Beer or Wine Bottle Without an Opener

We had an almost perfect setup on that ninety-degree afternoon. Five miles of cool and wild river lay in front of us, just enough tubes for each person with one left over for the beer bottles, nestled in a cooler full of ice. Not a cloud in the sky, not a worry in the world.

We were only about a quarter-mile downstream when we found out the bottles we had just purchased weren't of the "twist-off" variety. Suddenly five miles seemed a lot longer.

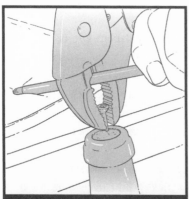

Use a drywall screw, vice-grips, and a screwdriver to mimic the fulcrum system of a typical cork puller. Screw-in coat or planter hooks also work well, as long as they're sturdy enough to withstand the strain.

I usually keep a bottle opener on my key chain, but none of us had anything more than our bathing suits on. We didn't despair, however; we quickly found out that by hooking the caps together and pulling hard, we were able to free at least one cap at a time. That worked twenty-three times—the last bottle rode all the way to the landing with us.

Usually all you need to open a beer bottle is to rest the edge of the cap against a hard surface and hit it sharply with the heel of your hand. The cap will scar wood, so don't try this on your oak table.

Wine bottles are a slightly more difficult proposition. If you don't have a cork puller, you can twist a screw into the cork (the wider the threads the better) and use pliers to pull on the screw and remove the cork. This takes a bit of muscle—traditional wine openers don't operate on a fulcrum system for nothing. If you don't have pliers or a screwdriver handy, a "coat hanger" screw (usually brass, threaded on one end and curved on the other; a lot of times they're also used to hang plants from ceilings) can be twisted in and pulled out by hand. Use a screwdriver and a countertop as an improvised fulcrum system. This system works with both traditional and plastic corks.

SECTION 6

Cooking

Corn on the Grill

Well, we better get the vegetables out of the way.

Actually, no summer BBQ is complete without some grilled sweet corn, which tastes far superior to boiled ears. The high heat of the grill tends to caramelize the sugars in the corn, and the smoke flavor often penetrates right into the kernels. The problem with cooking corn on the grill is twofold: It tends to dry out, and the ears take up a lot of space. The good news is you can grill the ears beforehand, yet still have them hot and moist when the steaks are done.

Use a cooler to soak the unhusked ears in clean water before grilling (keep the husks on throughout the entire process). You may need to place clean rocks or bricks on top of the ears to get them fully immersed. Let the ears soak for about an hour, then place them on the grill on medium-high heat. Dump the water out of the cooler, but don't wipe it dry. Rotate the ears once at about eight minutes, or when the grill-side husks start to brown. Cook for another six to eight minutes, then put them back in the damp cooler and close the lid.

Go ahead and grill the rest of your meal in leisure. The cooler will act as a steam bath, continuing to cook the ears at a high-humidity, low-heat setting. Just don't open the lid until you're ready to serve dinner, or that all-important steam will escape. The resulting corn will be moist, hot, and sweet.

 Grilling Steak

It's almost impossible to screw up a good steak on the grill. If you cook a decent-quality steak (porterhouse, T-bone, strip, or rib eye) anywhere from medium-rare up to medium-well, you need only a sprinkle of salt and pepper to enhance the natural flavor. The only real way to spoil a good steak is to overcook it, yet that happens a lot more than it should.

There are two theories on how to cook a steak on the grill: hot and fast or slow and steady. Hot and fast works great to seal in the juices while crisping the outside, resulting in a tender, juicy steak. This method involves slapping the steak down on the grill right above the flames, then cooking it for five to seven minutes on each side. The problem with direct grilling is that the heat on many grills is uneven, resulting in patches of steak being grilled to a crisp. It's also tough to get the inside cooked thoroughly, since the searing keeps the heat from penetrating to the middle of the steak.

Slow and steady cooking, or indirect grilling, will produce a more evenly cooked steak. Adherents of this method use an elevated rack, or just push the steaks to one side of the flames, and keep the lid closed to create an ovenlike environment. The problem with indirect grilling is that the juices often run off the steak as it heats, and you lose the char-ring and retention of natural juices that make a good grilled steak so flavorful.

The best way to get an evenly cooked steak with full flavor is to com-bine the two methods. Quickly sear the meat on each side for a min-ute or two to char the edges and seal in the juices. Then remove the steak from high heat with tongs—forks and skewers release juices when they puncture the meat—and allow it to finish cooking under indirect heat. Use a meat thermometer to make sure that each steak is cooked to the right temperature. Don't cut them open to check "doneness" since you'll lose juices and flavor. For a medium steak, the internal tempera-ture should be about 140–150°F.

Chefs routinely reserve the worst hunks of meat for those custom-ers who order well-done steaks. The reason for this is simple; you can't taste flavor in a well-done steak like you can with a medium-rare steak.

Drying out a perfectly good hunk of meat on your grill, then slathering it with artificial juices like steak sauce or—God forbid—ketchup is a total waste of the poor cow that died for your heathen appetite. At least try your steak cooked medium. If you can't bring yourself to try some pink meat, just buy some tofu for your next BBQ. It's cheaper, and will taste about the same.

If you're working with tougher cuts, there are a few simple household marinades to loosen up even the stringiest piece of beef. Cola, red wine, lemon juice, and vinegar can all be used to tenderize tough cuts. Just add equal amounts of water and allow the steak to marinate overnight. Italian dressing works wonders for naturally dry cuts, and is an excellent marinade for venison, which lacks the marbled fat of beef.

A clean grate helps keep the meat from sticking and tearing. Wipe a little vegetable oil over the grill, or just rub a crosscut spud over the grates for a nonstick cooking surface. The spud trick is a great way to keep campfire grates clean when you're away from home, too.

96　Deep-frying a Turkey

The days of hot kitchens, big roasting pans, and dried-out turkey have gone the way of the dodo. Deep-frying a turkey takes a quarter of the time that conventional methods do, and it produces a juicier, more flavorful bird. And once you try a deep-fried gobbler, you'll never cook a turkey in the oven again.

Turkey deep-frying is strictly an outdoor activity, but you don't want to do this on your wooden deck. Oil tends to leak out of the pot, and it's tough to get the resulting stain out of the boards. To determine the level of oil to add, put the turkey in the pot and add enough water to totally immerse the bird, then pull the turkey back out. The resulting water level marks the amount of oil needed. Empty the water and fill with oil, and pat the turkey dry. Place the pot on a propane burner and start heating the oil.

To avoid burning the bird, or soaking it in lukewarm oil before cooking, you need to put it in at exactly the right time. To determine the perfect oil temperature, just toss an unlit match into the oil. Once it ignites, go ahead and lower the turkey into the just-right oil using a wire holder. This trick works great to check oil temperature for any kind of deep-frying.

Now all you have to do is let the turkey cook for about forty-five minutes, or until the thigh joint reaches a temperature of 165°F. Then carefully remove the turkey from the hot oil, shut the burner off, and allow the turkey to drip-dry and cool down for five to ten minutes.

Injected marinades, either store-bought or homemade, can really spice up the relatively bland breast meat. Work the injector through different layers of muscles before cooking, and don't be shy about adding too much marinade. Much of it will leak back out during the cooking process, but what remains will make for some flavorful eating.

97 Drunken Chicken

Not only does this sound cool, but it's also the best way to cook a whole bird on the grill. Plus, you have to crack a beer to cook drunken chicken, and beers are sorta like potato chips; you can't stop at just one. You have to sip a cold brew or two while the bird cooks (it's an unwritten law). Another great part about drunken chicken is that you don't have to constantly tend it. The beer does the cooking for you. Whoever thought this up is my hero.

For the best flavor, season the chicken well both inside and out. Putting the chicken in a large bag with spices and shaking it works great, but you'll want to do it outside. Women tend to get a little ornery about paprika-laced chicken juice flying around the kitchen. Now stuff a small potato or onion in the neck hole of the chicken, and pull the skin flap over it. This will help keep the steam inside the bird. Finally, crack open a beer and drink about one-third to half of it—never use a full beer when cooking drunken chicken. A full beer will boil over, dousing the coals and—even worse—ruining ounces of perfectly drinkable beer. Set the beer in a commercially available "drunken chicken" can holder—about $2, then set the chicken down on top of the beer, arse first. The beer steam will slowly work into the chicken.

You'll want to be able to close the grill lid, so buy a small enough chicken. A charcoal grill gives a superior taste compared to propane, but make sure to position the coals around the outside of the bird. It takes about an hour or two to cook a bird this way, but don't worry about being bored.

You've got the rest of that twelve-pack to keep you company.

 Smoking Fish

Back when I used to live in town, there was one surefire way to meet the neighbors. Every Labor Day I would fire up my smoker and, over the course of the entire day, smoke the accumulated trout, salmon, and catfish I had caught over the summer. A cooler of cold beer and a radio ensured a steady stream of visitors, some of whom I barely knew—at the start of the day.

There isn't a store-bought herring in the world that can compare to hot, freshly smoked fish, and smoking is deceptively simple. You don't need a special smoker, although they're very nice: A regular gas or charcoal grill works almost as well. It's a time-consuming practice, but also easy and strangely fulfilling. I'm certain one of my ancestors was one of those simple cavemen who could stare at a fire all night without blinking.

Fatty fish work best for smoking. Trout, salmon, catfish, sturgeon, herring, and a variety of rough fish (suckers, carp, etc.) are common freshwater candidates for the smoker. Cod, mackerel, and halibut are often used for smoking on the coasts. Whatever you use, catch or buy them fresh (within a couple of months at most), since fish that are frozen for long periods tend to suffer protein breakdown and take brine too easily, resulting in salty fish. You should leave the skin on, but if you have only skinless fillet you can just slip a piece of aluminum foil underneath the meat during the smoking process.

Brining is one of the essential parts of smoking. Many old-timers used to throw in liberal amounts of salt; the adage was to use enough salt to float an egg (things are more buoyant in salt water than fresh water). Today, with modern refrigerators, that amount of preservative isn't necessary. I use about a half-cup of canning salt (iodine-free) per gallon of water, along with some brown sugar, soy sauce, and fruit juice, but all you really need is the salt. Steak the fish or fillet them, leaving the bones in and skin on. Then soak the fish in the brine about twelve hours.

The fire used for smoking fish has to be, well, smoky. Start a good fire with dry wood, then let it burn down to the coals. Add green (freshly cut or soaked in water) wood on top of the coals, which will produce low heat and enough smoke to cause the neighbors to remove their delicates from the clothesline. If you're using a propane grill, use the lowest possible setting and just one burner, saving the coolest side for the fish. Many places sell metal boxes for wood chips that are designed specifically for propane grills.

Alder or fruit-tree (apple, plum, etc.) wood produces a mild, flavorful smoke. Mesquite and hickory produce a sharper smoke. Soaking the wood chips before use helps produce more smoke, no matter what kind of wood chip you buy or gather.

Heat is your enemy here, at least to start with; high heat sears the outer edges of the fish and doesn't let the smoky flavor work into the flesh. Don't put the fish in the smoker until you've got the temperature down to about 140–160°F. Smoke the fish at this temperature for roughly six to eight hours, or until the meat has browned and is just beginning to flake. Then bring the temperature up to 180–200°F for an hour to kill any parasites. Heat can be controlled by standard methods, either by adjusting air intake or fuel load. Don't shut down the smoke outlet though; this causes the smoke to sour and produces a bitter flavor in the fish.

Smoked fish lasts a long time in the refrigerator. It's usually best to make it in large batches, considering the amount of time involved. It makes a good gift, too; wrap it in wax paper and newspaper and people will invariably ask where you bought that incredible smoked fish.

One word of caution: If you're using your regular grill for smoking, the oils from the fish may accumulate on the bottom of the grill or smoker and cause whatever you cook next to taste fishy. To eliminate this, line the bottom of the grill with aluminum foil beforehand. When you're done smoking fish, remove the foil and start a hot, clean (no smoking chips) fire. That should take care of all or most of the fishy smell.

99 Seasoning and Cleaning a Cast-iron Skillet

Over the years I've eaten many memorable shore lunches, little impromptu meals cooked over an open fire near the water's edge. Invariably these meals include freshly caught fish, good company, and a battered old cast-iron skillet. The food that comes out of these skillets rarely disappoints, and the skillets themselves are darn near indestructible. Sadly, these old-style pans have given way to stainless steel and Teflon-coated cookware, despite the fact that cast-iron skillets hold a steadier heat and are even easier to clean than modern nonstick pans.

The key to using a new cast-iron pan is the seasoning process. Simply coat the inside of the pan with an animal-based fat, such as lard or bacon grease, and bake in the oven (or over a campfire) for about a half hour at 350°F. Remove the pan, dump out the grease and bake it for a couple more hours. Allow it to cool, then wipe dry with a rag or paper towel. Do not clean the pan with detergents or abrasive pads, which will ruin the coating you just applied. Also avoid cooking acidic foods such as tomatoes or citrus fruits, which can cause the skillet to rust. Stick with high-fat, greasier foods for the first few uses. This usually isn't a problem on most camping trips.

Cleaning a cast-iron skillet is so simple it seems wrong, or at least unhygienic. But all you need to do is fill it with hot water after you're done cooking, let it heat up a bit, then wipe it clean. Again, don't use detergents or abrasive pads, both of which will strip away that unique coating.

Hang the pan or store it upside-down to prevent rust. If you do see rust pockets, just warm up the pan and scour it clean (okay, okay—*now* you can use an abrasive pad), then reseason it. Old, nasty-looking rusty cast-iron skillets found at garage sales aren't necessarily ruined, or even damaged; you simply need to clean it up and reseason it.

 Pickling Fish

Pickling fish is another old tradition that dates back to the prerefrigeration age. While modern refrigeration makes pickling unnecessary for preservation purposes, pickled fish has a distinctive, pleasing flavor, and the acid in the pickling brine will dissolve bones, which means fine filleting of those bony fish isn't necessary.

In the refrigerator, soak one-inch cubes of skinned fish in a brine solution containing two cups of kosher salt (no iodine) per one gallon of water overnight. Rinse the fish and add the chunks to a large pot of water containing about five cups of water and two quarts of distilled vinegar. Add onions, garlic, allspice, mustard seed, cloves, and pepper for flavor (add more spices as desired—it's tough to ruin pickled fish), then bring it all to a simmer for fifteen minutes. Do not cold-pickle fish unless you want to risk having a tapeworm take up residence in your intestinal tract. While the tapeworm diet undoubtedly has Atkins beat, there's still that twenty-foot tapeworm to battle once you reach your fighting weight.

Take the fish out of the pot and place on a cookie sheet, and then put the chunks in the refrigerator to cool. Strain the pot of boiling vinegar with a colander or cheesecloth, then discard the spices and set the liquid aside. Pack the fish cubes in clean, sterilized (boiled) glass jars, adding more onions, garlic, and maybe a bay leaf or a wedge of lemon. Bring the strained stock back up to a boil, and then pour it over the fish cubes. Seal the jars, then refrigerate for a few weeks. Serve with crackers, lots of cold beer, and a fishing yarn or two.

(101) Beef Jerky

Few edible items are as beloved by guys as a hunk of salty, dried beef. Yet store-bought jerky is often loaded with preservatives and can be expensive if you're planning on supplying enough for a group of guys at a card party or on a weekend fishing trip. The good news is you can make lots of jerky at home, with no special equipment, and at a fraction of the cost of the stuff sold in the store.

Start out by buying the right kind of meat. You'll want a low-fat cut with bigger muscle groups; round steaks or rump roasts are perfect. Most wild game is naturally low-fat and makes excellent jerky, including deer, elk, and even filleted goose breasts. If the meat is frozen, don't defrost it all the way. Partially frozen meat is much easier to slice into thin strips.

Cut across the grain of the meat with a sharp knife, trimming away fat or connective tissue. The strips should be about a quarter-inch thick and pure muscle. Jerky shrinks when it cooks, so it's easy to underestimate the amount of meat you need. A good-sized rump roast will only give enough jerky to fill a plastic baggie.

Now marinate the meat in either a homemade or commercial brine. Store-bought mixes are fine, but homemade mixes are more fun and just as tasty. You can use a base marinade of two cups of salt per gallon of water, then add different ingredients, mixing and matching spices to match your own tastes. Like hot and sweet jerky? Add brown sugar and cayenne pepper. Prefer peppered strips? Add cracked black and red peppers. Straight soy sauce makes a great marinade, too, either alone or with a combination of other marinades. Remember to keep the salt level constant; that is, if you add soy sauce, subtract some salt from the brine.

Marinate overnight in the fridge, then place the strips in the dehydrator or in the oven. If you use the oven, set the strips on the grating or on aluminum foil over the top of a cookie sheet, then bake at the lowest setting and crack the door to help the dehydration process. You can also smoke jerky, but avoid smokers that have been used to smoke fish.

It's easy to overcook jerky, since the meat will continue to lose moisture after you remove it from heat and can quickly become brittle. Six to eight hours will usually dry out most strips of jerky. One of the most common mistakes is waiting for the jerky to become brittle; the meat can lose up to 25 percent more moisture after it's removed from the heat source.

Some Food for Thought

Well, that's it. No theories for nuclear fission or world peace, but some fun and, hell, maybe even important things to try.

If something does work out for you, pass it along. Damn near every thing in this book I've learned from other people. Some of the lessons weren't much fun, while others went down so smooth I wasn't even aware I was being taught. Those are the ones I remember fondly.

It's not a contest, with the guy who knows the most being the biggest man. If you can slip somebody a tip or two when he's in a jam, and do it in a gracious manner, then you're going to have that person's quiet but deep respect, and probably for a long, long time. I know I reserve a special part in my heart for the guys and gals who've brought me through some thick tangles with a smile and a nod, and I try to emulate that whenever I can.

It's not always easy, but it feels right when you do it. More than right; it feels like the sort of thing a real guy would do. A real good guy.

So stick together out there. We're all stupid at one time or another, and we're all competent other times. We just don't hit all of our low notes at the same time . . . and we sure as hell don't hit the high ones all that often, either. No matter what we tell each other over beers, no matter how confident we appear, at times our world can be as confusing and dark as that old shuttered garage. I hope this sheds a little bit of light, and makes those dark days a little bit brighter. If not, well, refer back to the beer bong chapter. Find the light where you can, even if it's light beer.

Section 6: Cooking

Keep on keeping on, brothers.
Peace.

The End

INDEX

Index

Index

Index

Index